I0753660

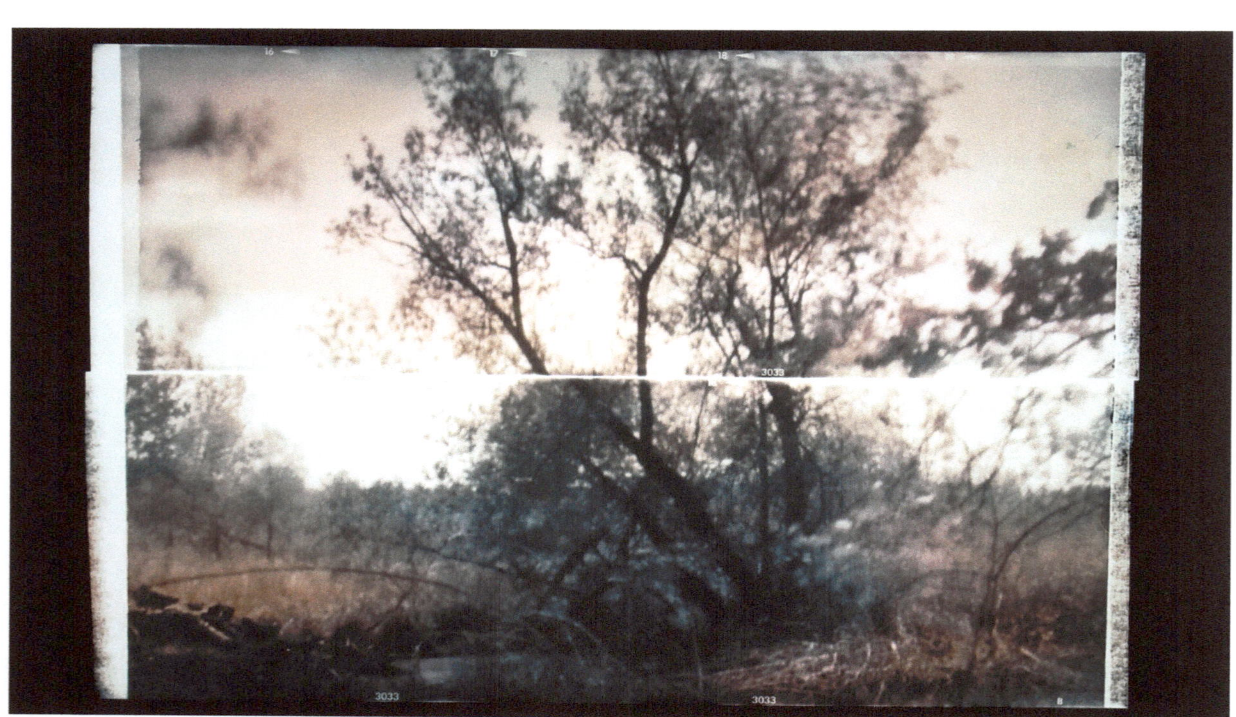

Day's End

Mark L. Eshbaugh

Introduction by John C. Tremblay

For more information about the artist visit http://www.markeshbaugh.com
For more information about John C. Tremblay visit http://www.ratrilpot.com
For more information on all RMR Press publications visit our website at:
http://www.rmr-press.com

First Edition

10 9 8 7 6 5 4 3 2 1
Printed in the United States of America

ISBN-13: 978-0-6151-5262-2

Introduction

In otherworld mythology, the day's end is that time when the border between this world and the otherworld becomes thin—bestowing upon mortals a glimpse of what is normally hidden behind the veil and allowing otherworldly creatures to play in our realm.

When I look at this aptly titled collection of Mark Eshbaugh's photographs, I begin to wonder if he might have a bit of otherwordly blood in his veins. For like the sprites that cross the borders, he has the power to pique our attention, whisper to us in riddles, tickle our imaginations, and instill curiosity as intense as that in childhood, all the while reminding us that the true world is just beyond our senses.

Yet strangely enough, even though we can never accurately see reality through a photograph, these images somehow allow us to transcend what technology, biology, and time itself strives to hide from us. By viewing the image with our eyes, hearts, and minds, we can experience that crystal clear moment when all the pieces of the day fall into place… that split second where despite how chaotic the world is around us, we find ourselves awestruck and humbled by a simple hush… a sense of inner peace… a taste of serenity.

It's a contradiction of course. How can an image of a raging storm be serene? Look at the photographs. Mark shows you how. He captures the essence of that moment… that setting… that emotion. He shows us what is beyond the trees, above the clouds, beneath the water, and within the winds. All it takes for us to go there is to surrender to the trickster and follow him on a journey.

And so we do follow, almost helplessly, through fractured images and subtle colors that remind us of the wonders that can only be seen by drinking in the intoxicating aromas of the proverbial rose. Each image is a single perfect flower and together their fragrances combine to become something greater than what they could be alone… a memory that burns into the consciousness… remaining with you until the end of your days.

But what about the medium? What about the tape and the arrows, the lines and the words, the panes and the numbers? Don't these things call attention to themselves? Don't they sit up and scream… LOOK AT ME! I SHOULDN'T BE HERE! Don't they detract from the collective vision he is lulling us to dream?

Not at all. Mark's hand-crafted cameras are instruments of magic, treasures that frame the intensity of the moment with word pictures from the world in which we live. We know words. We know numbers. We know symbols. The medium is the bardsong that Mark uses to communicate with us. And in doing so, Mark has achieved success in an area that artists have struggled since days of old. Not only are each of his seemingly mystical images works of art; they are works of art that incorporate the medium they are composed in. Magritte's La Trahison Des Images with its inspiring catchphrase "Ceci n'est pas une pipe" comes to mind. This is not a landscape, this is an image of a landscape.

Through purposeful design, he takes us by the hand and shows us how to make the most of our fleeting time on the borders of our realm. Here, look at the way the light is peeking through the branches and bubbling up from beneath the waters. Can you see that? No? Let me bring you that much closer to the fringe. Would color help? I can add it. Just a touch so that you can feel what's there. Ahh… that's better. How about over here too? Perfect. It's subtle enough so as not to make you question the truth, but powerful enough to speak to you of endless possibilities.

And as we hover by threshold, we can see how closely connected the physical destinations of our world truly are. Savannah Georgia and Carlisle Massachusetts aren't miles apart at the day's end… they're beside each other. Just look at the photograph. We can travel hundreds of miles—what would normally take hours upon hours—with one single step.

The choice is yours. Do you want to form walls and borders that prevent you from seeing the whole picture? Fine. Step up close to the diptychs, the triptych, or the nontych. The walls are there. Each image is separated out for you, so that you can glimpse only that snippet… only what you could fit within the tiny frame of what society has told you to accept for yourself.

But if you're braver... if you're energized from your brush with the mythical… if you think you can handle seeing more than what you're accustomed to… then take a step back. Allow the walls to fade away and the scene to unravel itself before your very eyes. There aren't two, three, or nine images. There is one scene overflowing off the paper and into your soul.

Alas… you must hurry. That window of opportunity at the day's end lasts but a few moments. And once the sun sets and the curtains have been drawn, another period of anxious waiting begins.

Yes you can go back again, when dusk begins to fall… but you will never again experience the moment as you did the first time. That's part of the magic, you see. Every time we return to these images, we come to them with a new perspective, freshened by the lessons of the new day. What was once a still glade, may now be a jungle waiting to be explored. What was once a dazzling display of nature's power, may now be chilling reminder of nature's fury. What was once a cold bleak landscape of sorrow is now a bright crisp unmarked field of hope. Only time and experience can say what the images will mean to you.

And when the journey is done, don't forget the soul who made your trip possible. The dreamweaver… the trickster… the creature of contradiction…. Mark Eshbaugh. Whether your adventure inspires you, thrills you, haunts you, or calms you; whether you concentrate on tiny fragments or swelling landscapes; and whether you look at these images for the first time or the hundredth time… it is Mark who is your guide and companion.

He used his gifts to create the one-of-a-kind cameras. He shared his visions and captured the one-of-a-kind moments. He mixed the potions that made the one-of-a-kind images.

Now go ahead and begin your trek to the threshold of our world, hand in hand with the man who hovers between worlds… weaving his magic… at the Day's End.

-John C. Tremblay

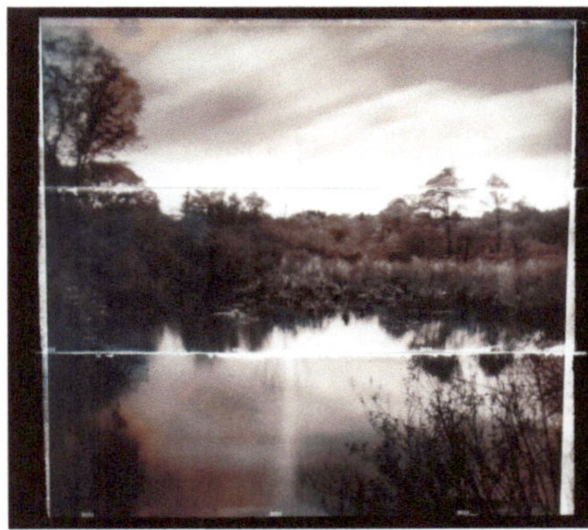

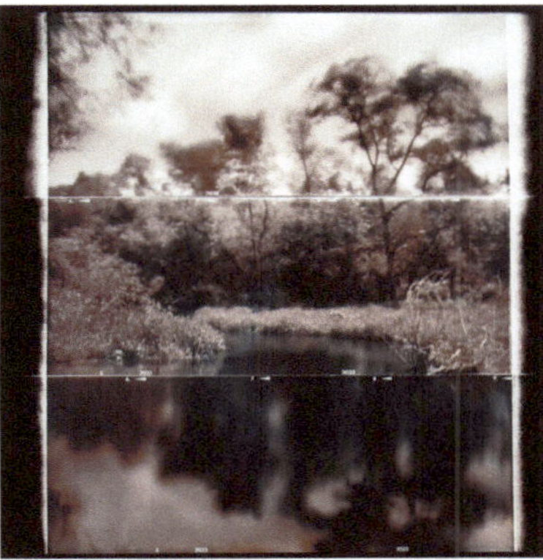

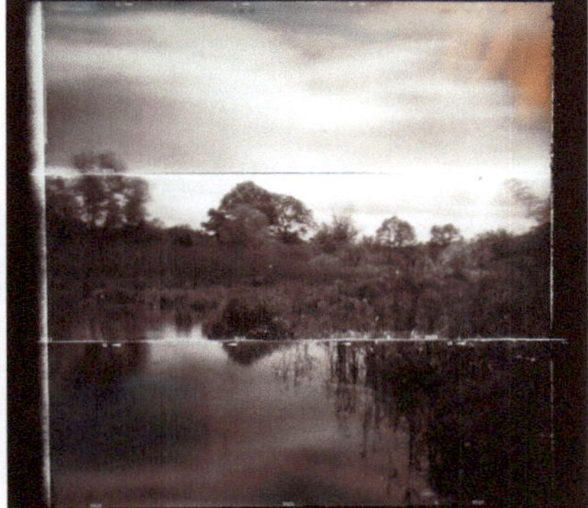

Day's End

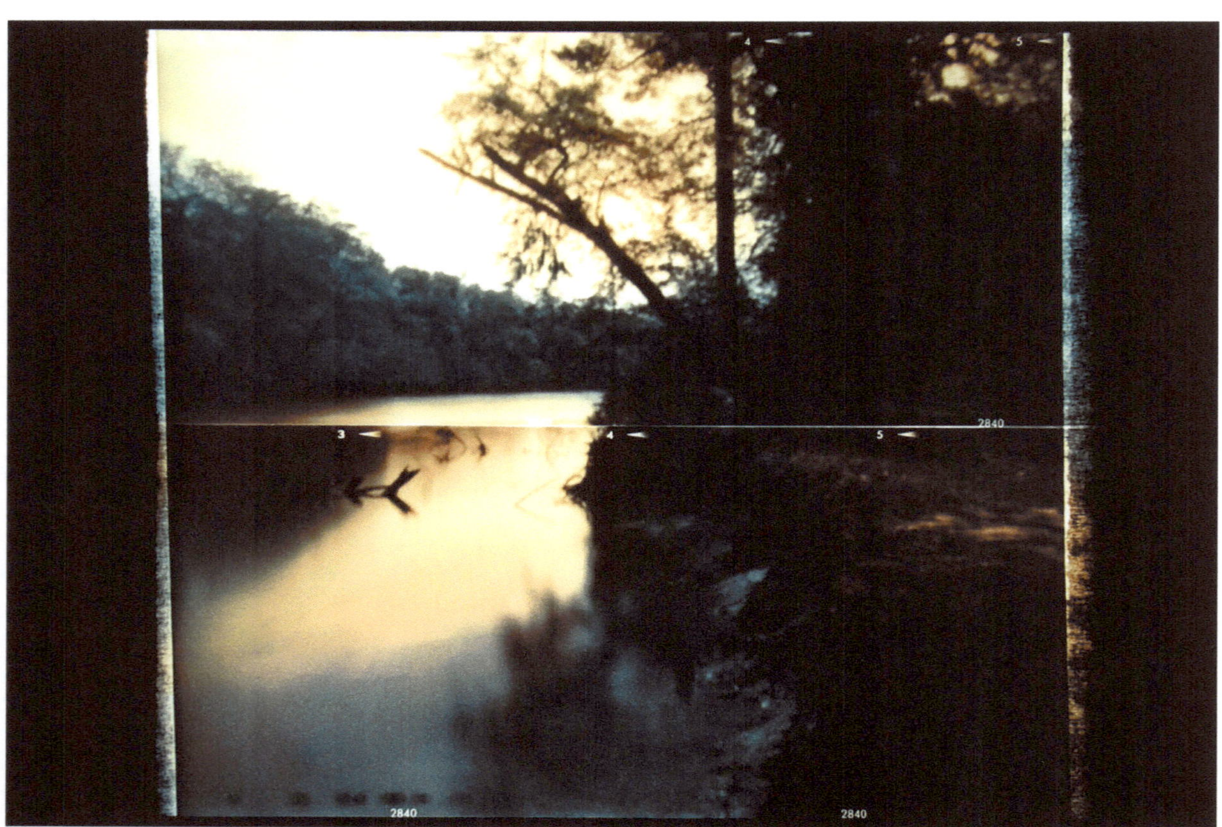
4
5
2840
3
4
5
2840
2840

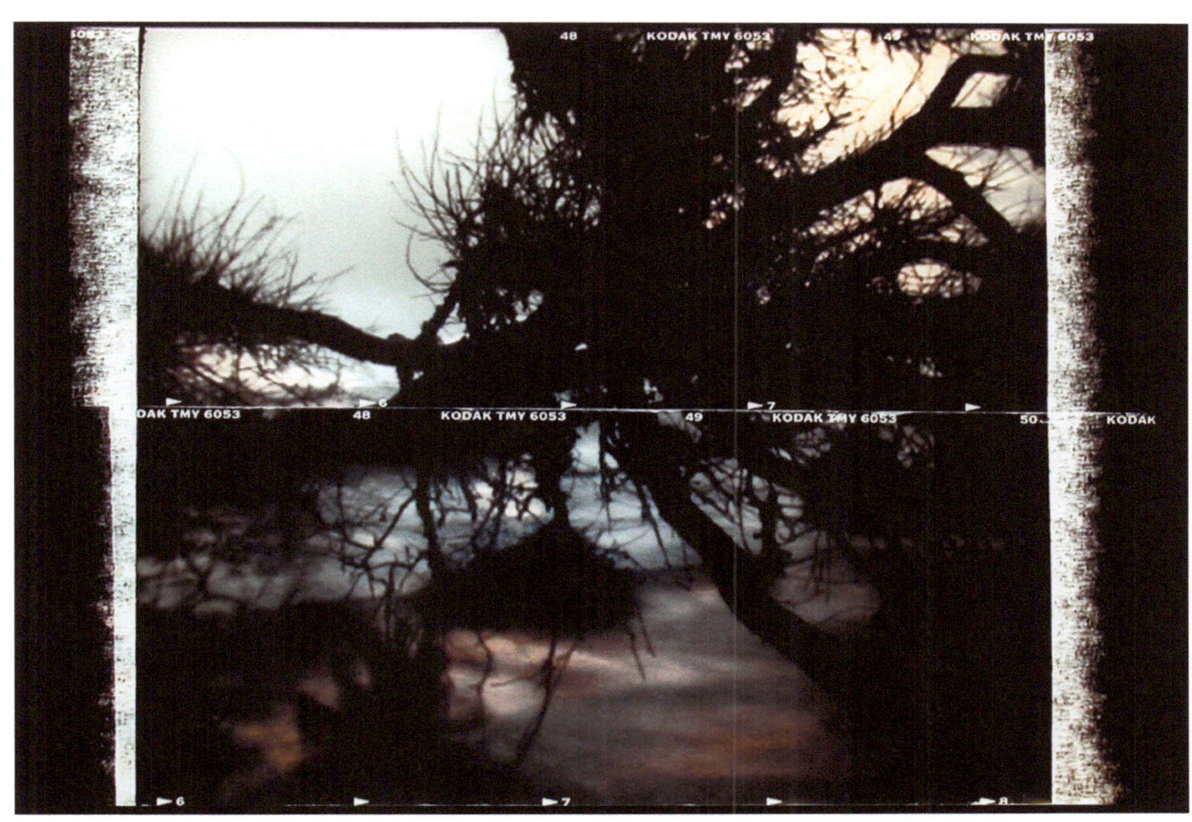

48
KODAK TMY 6053
KODAK TMY 6053
6
7
DAK TMY 6053
48
KODAK TMY 6053
49
KODAK TMY 6053
KODAK
6
7

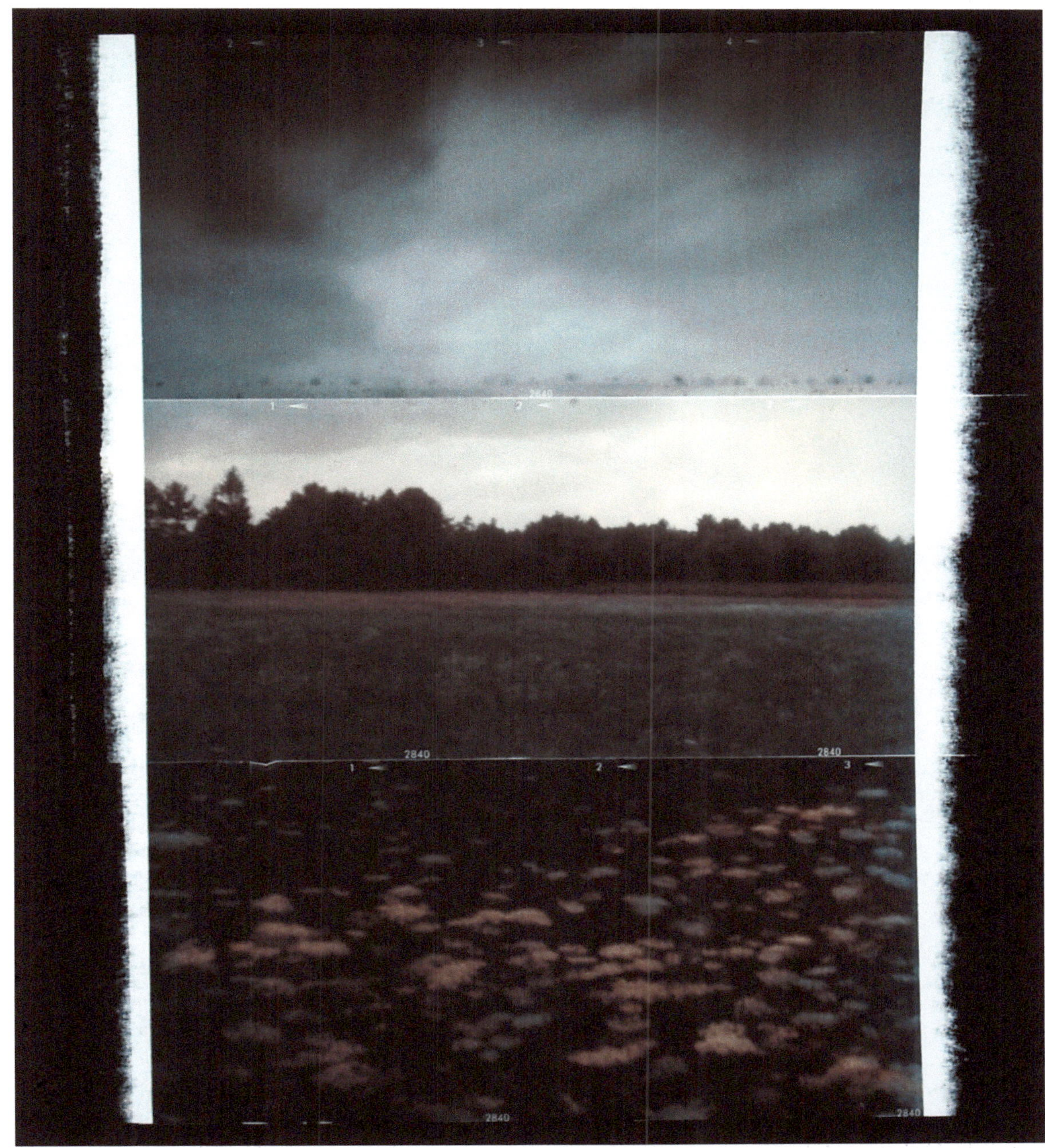

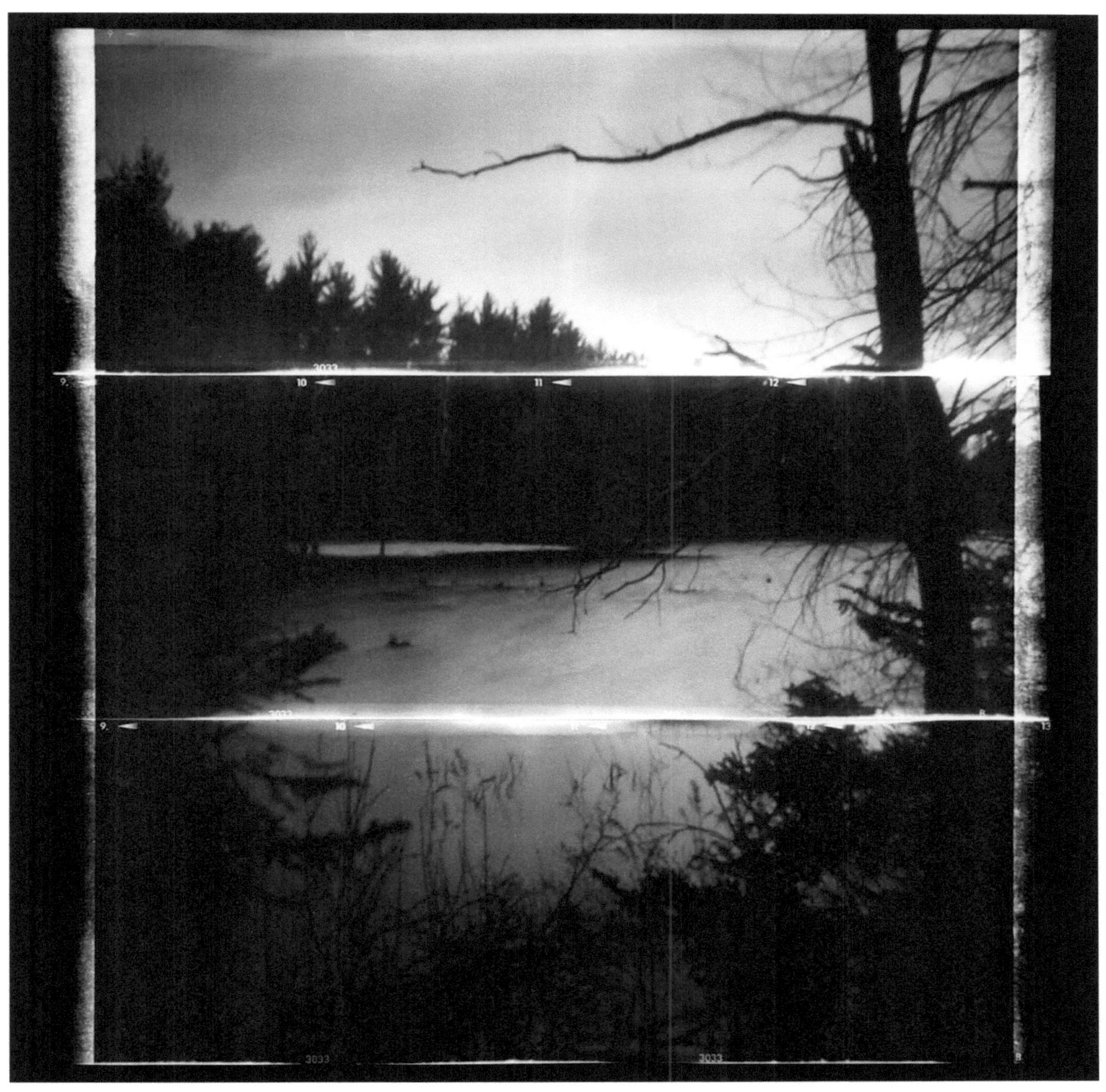

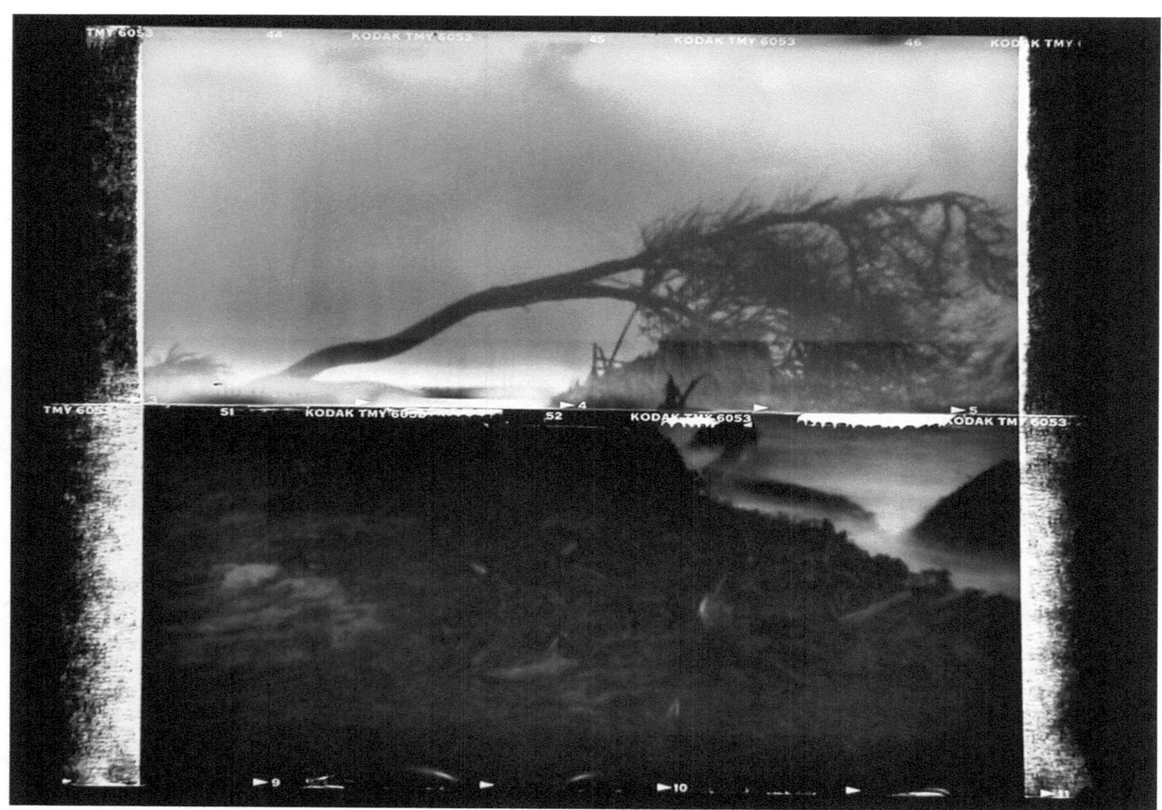
TMY 6053
44
KODAK TMY 6053
45
KODAK TMY 6053
46
51
52
KODAK TMY 6053

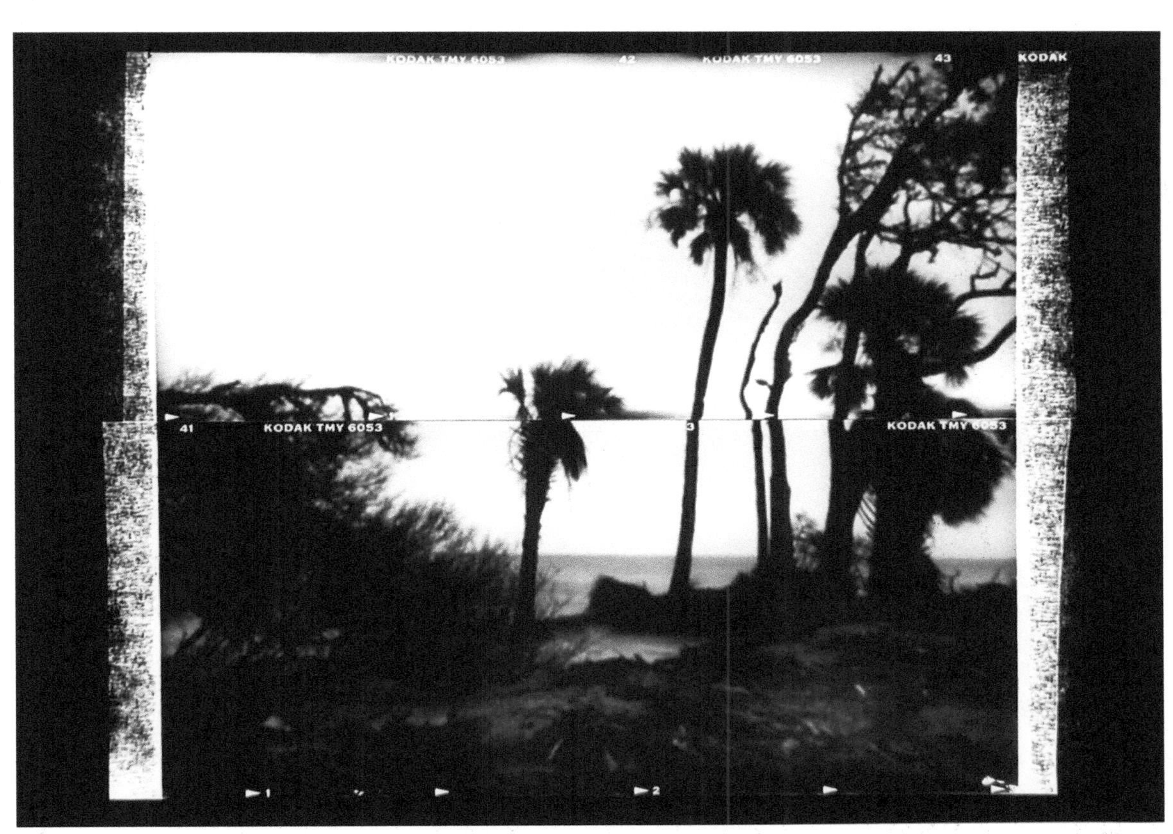
KODAK TMY 6053
42
KODAK TMY 6053
43
KODAK
41
KODAK TMY 6053
KODAK TMY 6053
1
2

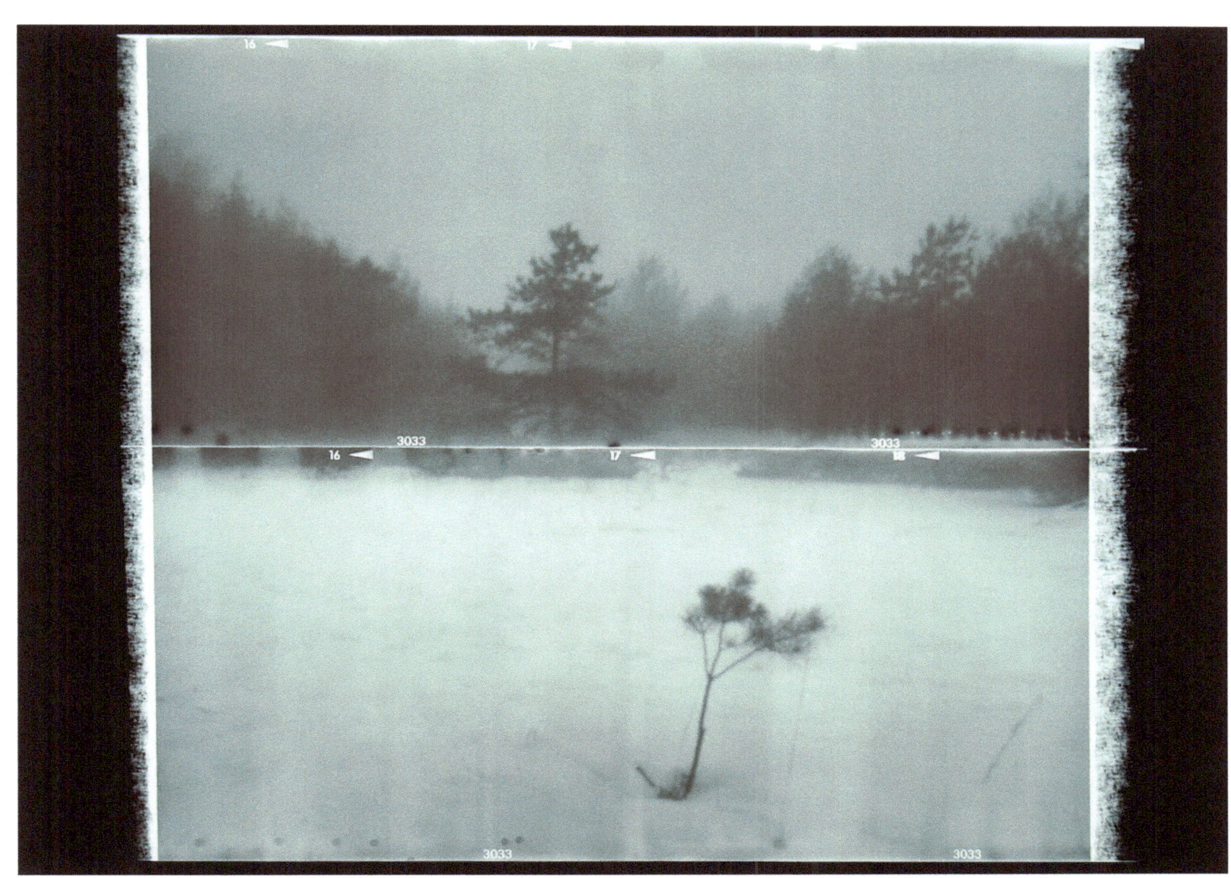
16
17
3033
3033
16
17
18
3033
3033

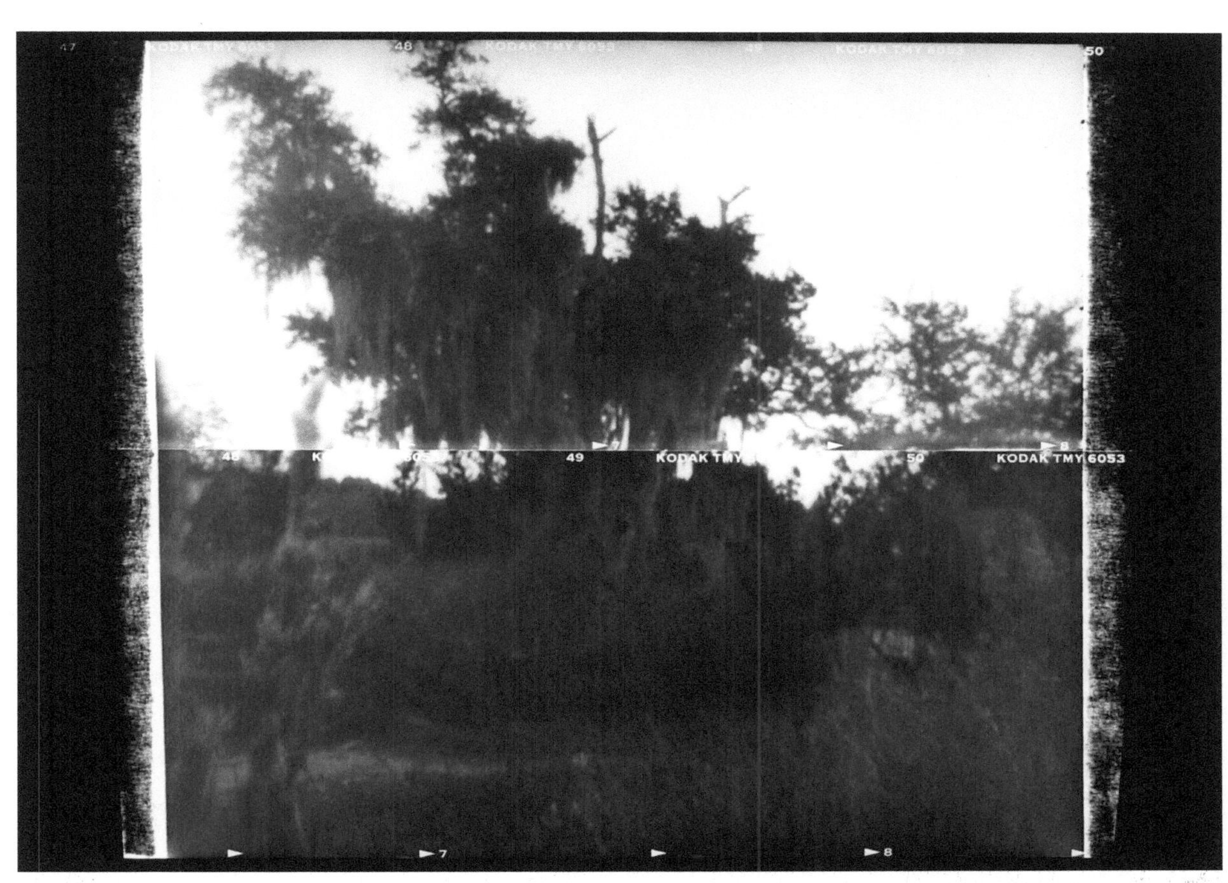
48
50
49
KODAK TMY
50
KODAK TMY 6053
►7
►8

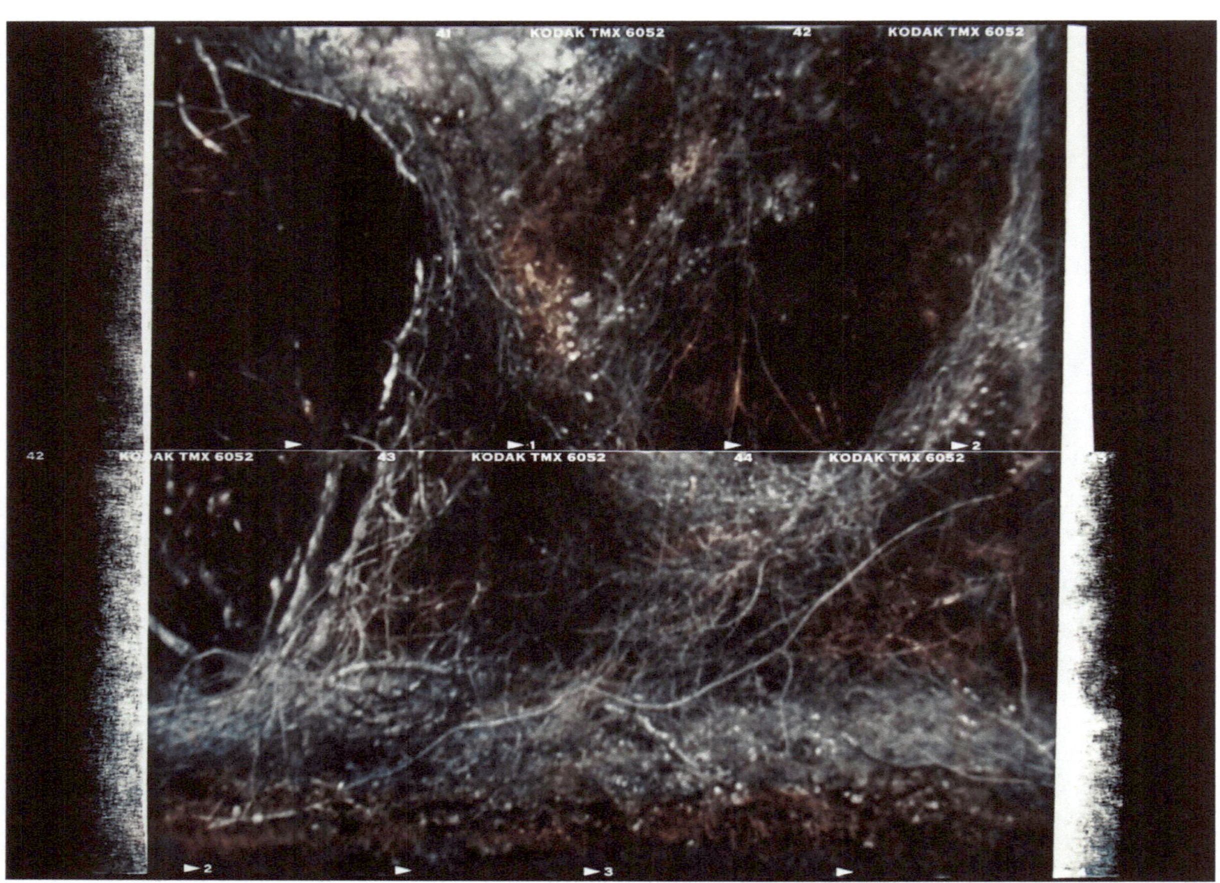
41
KODAK TMX 6052
42
KODAK TMX 6052
42
KODAK TMX 6052
43
KODAK TMX 6052
44
KODAK TMX 6052

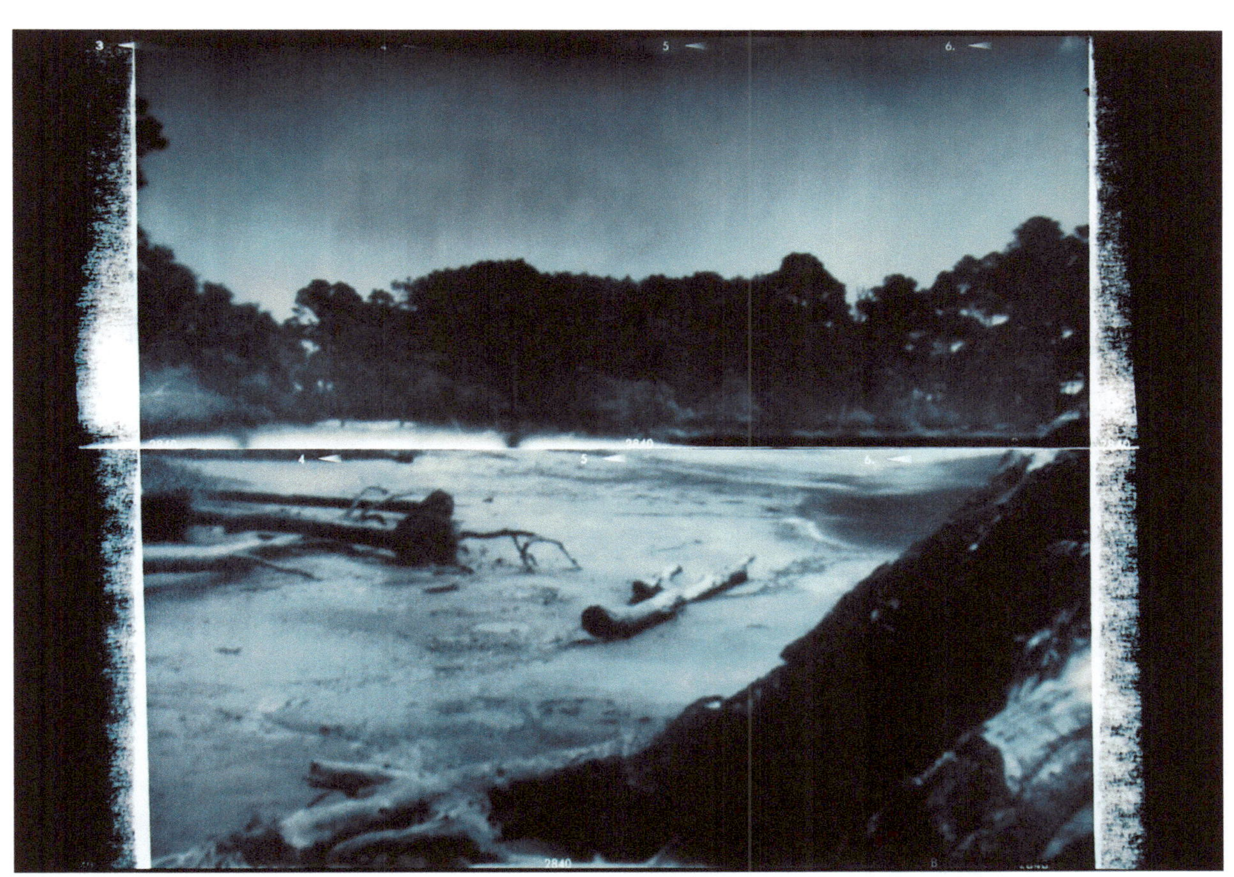

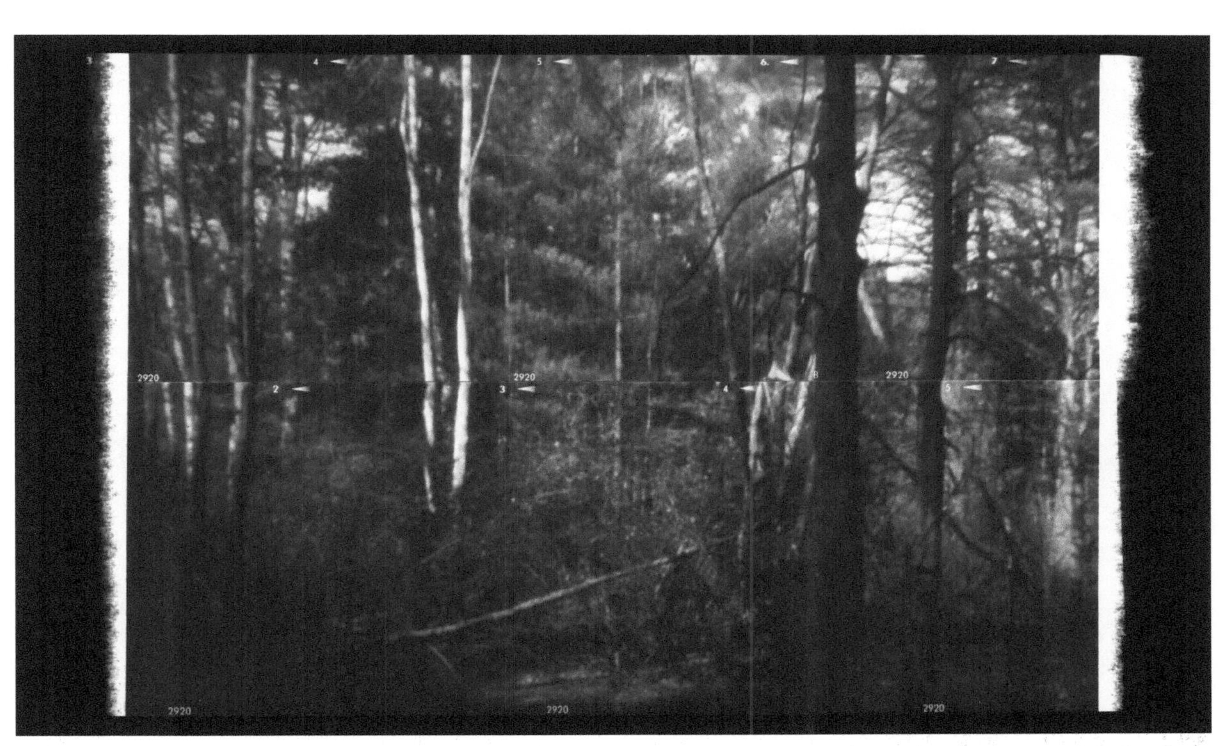

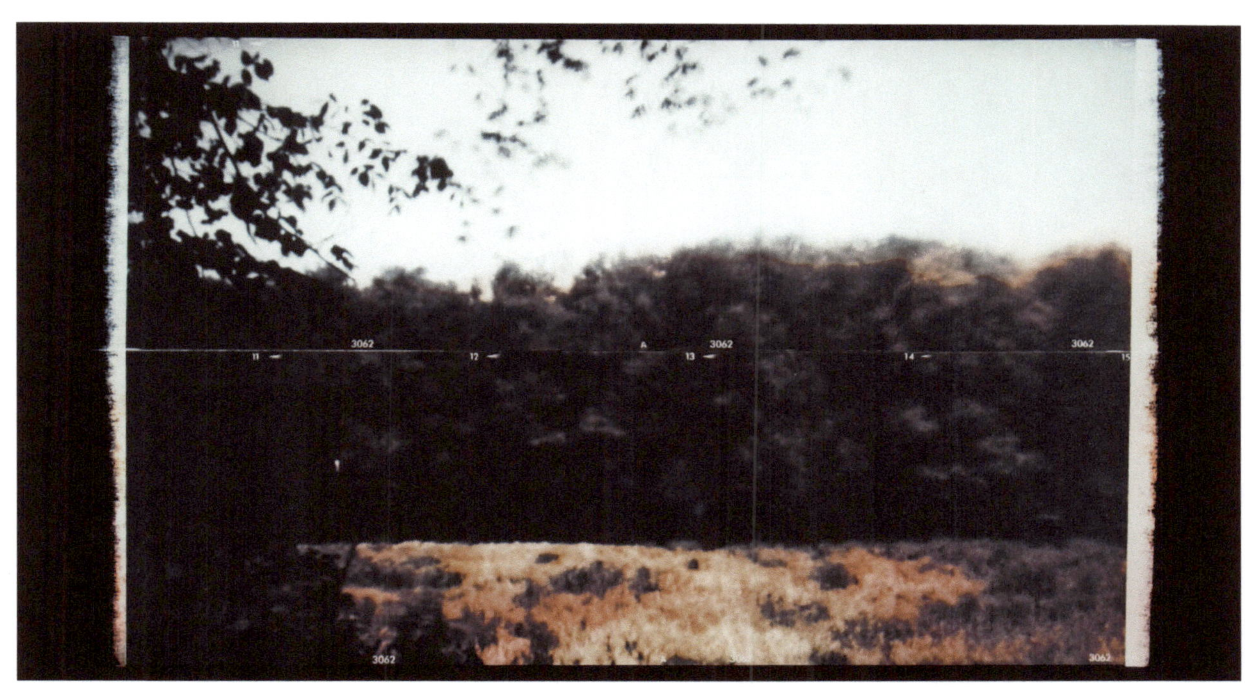
3062
A
3062
3062
11
12
13
14
15
3062
3062

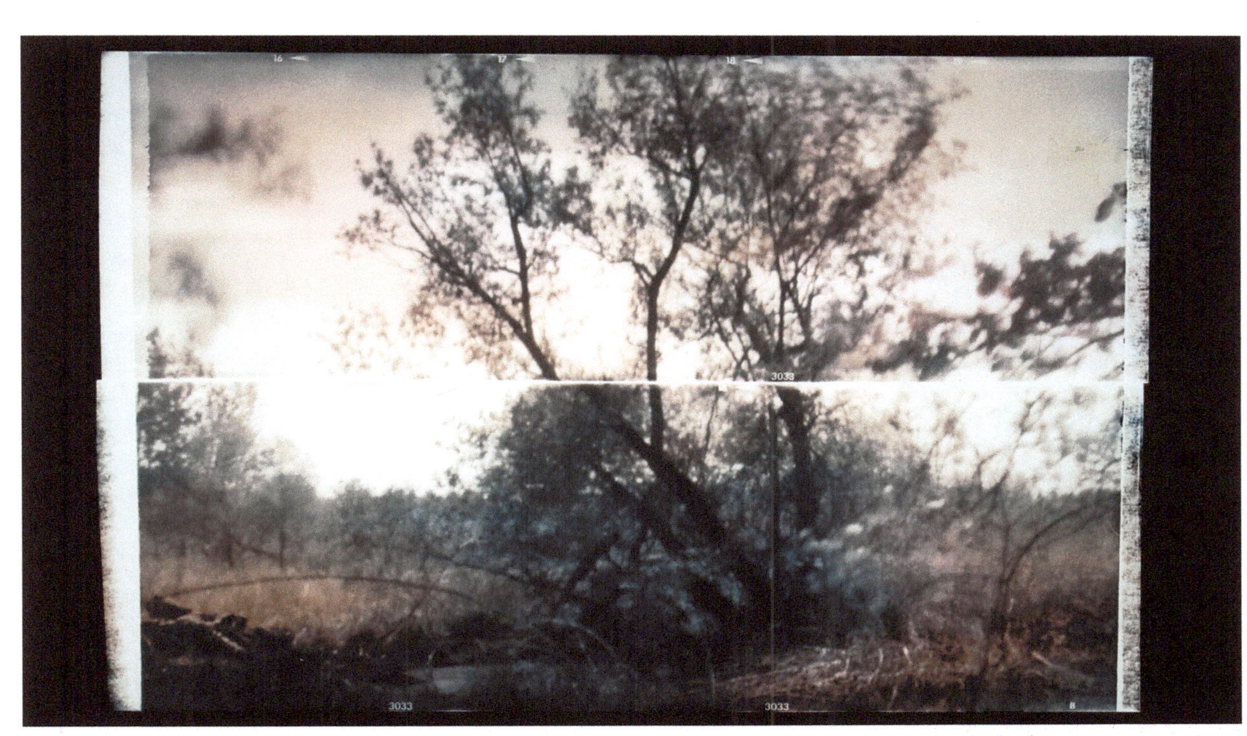

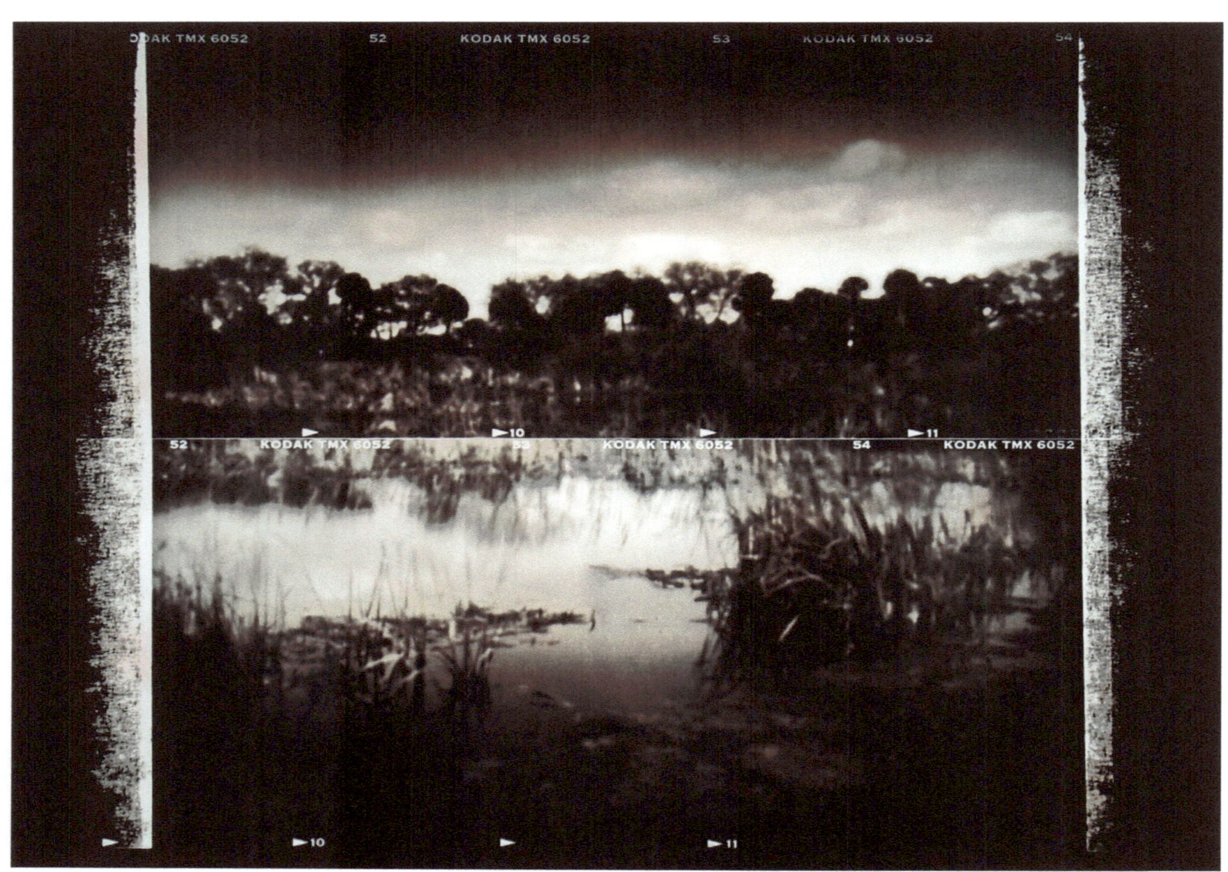
KODAK TMX 6052
52
KODAK TMX 6052
53
KODAK TMX 6052
54
10
11
52
KODAK TMX 6052
KODAK TMX 6052
54
KODAK TMX 6052
10
11

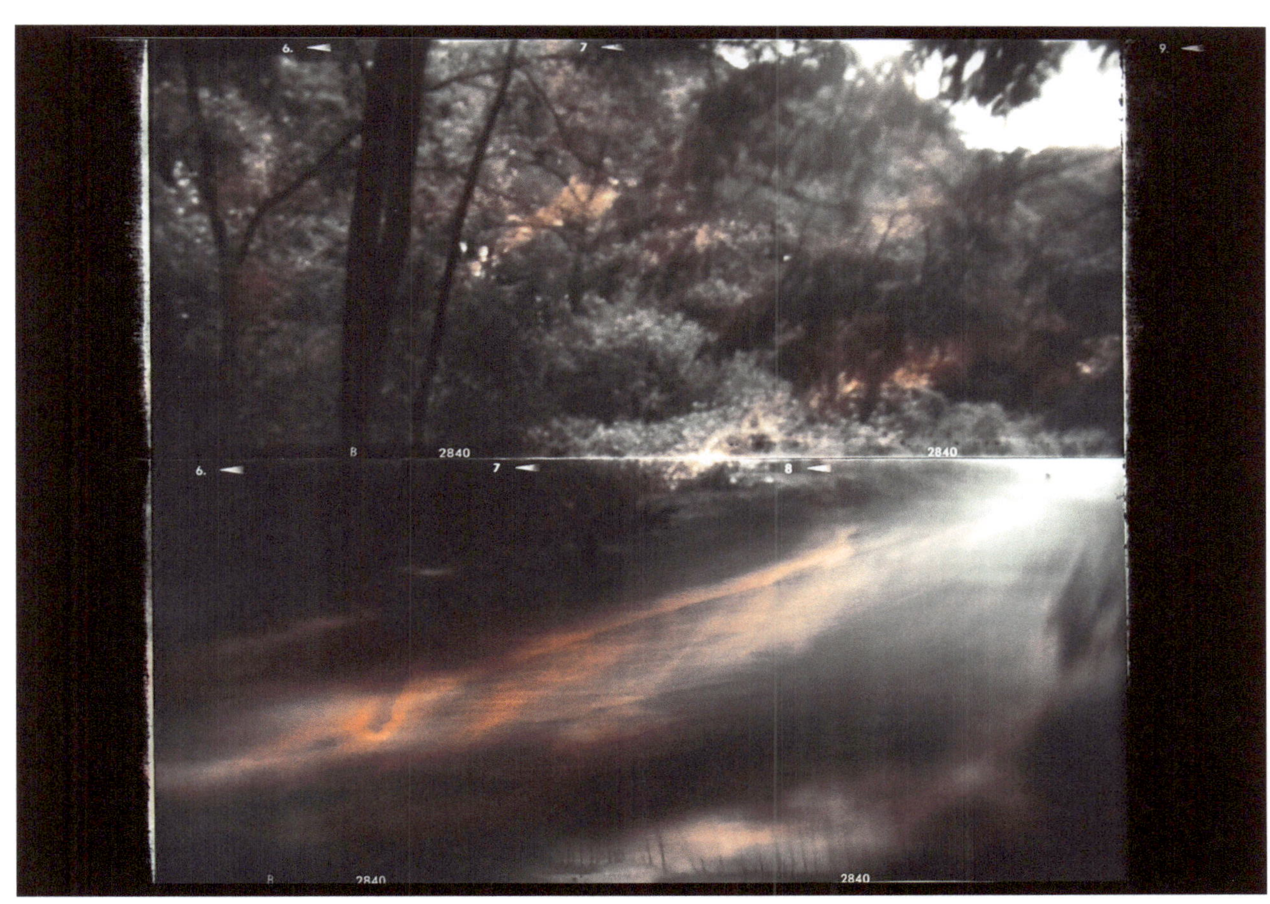
6.
7
9.
B
2840
2840
6.
7
8
B
2840
2840

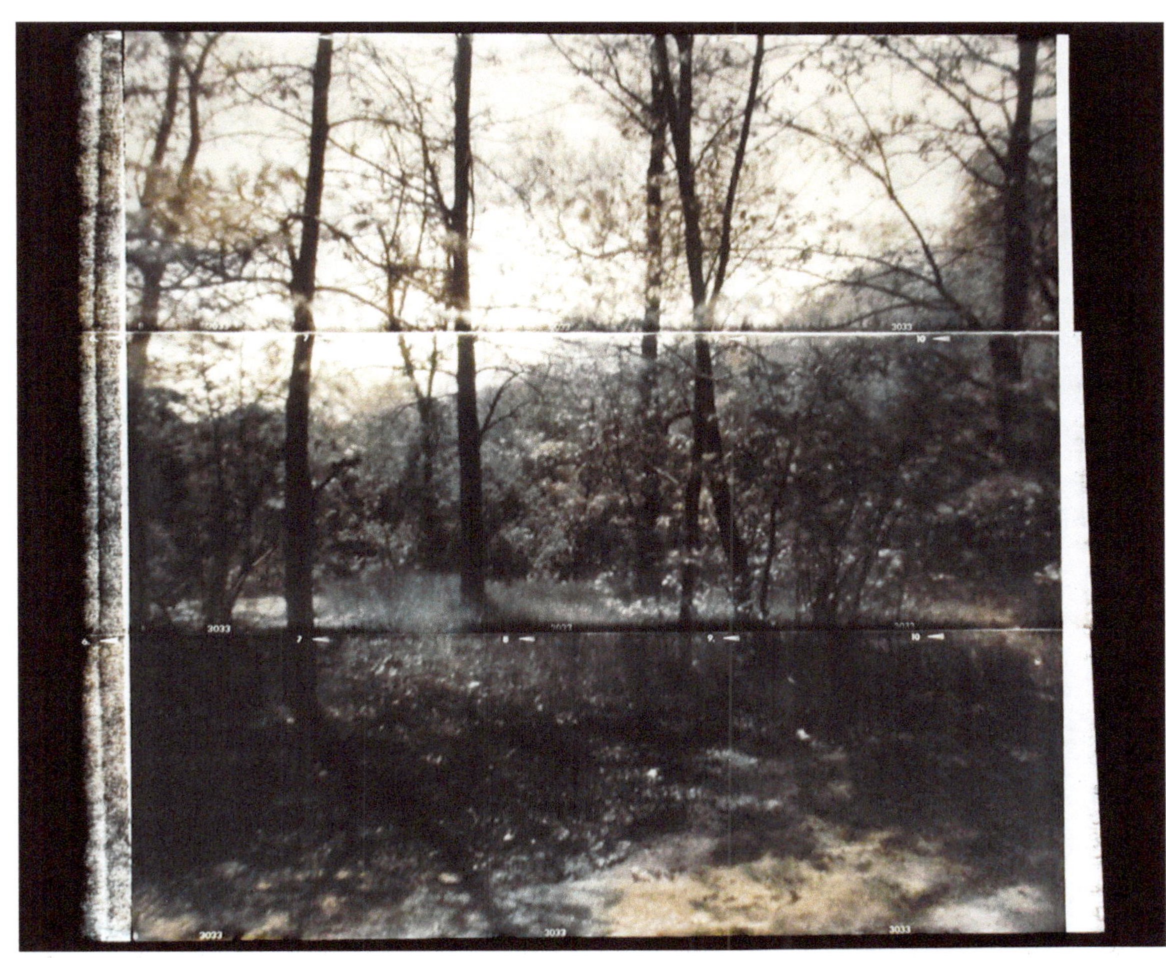

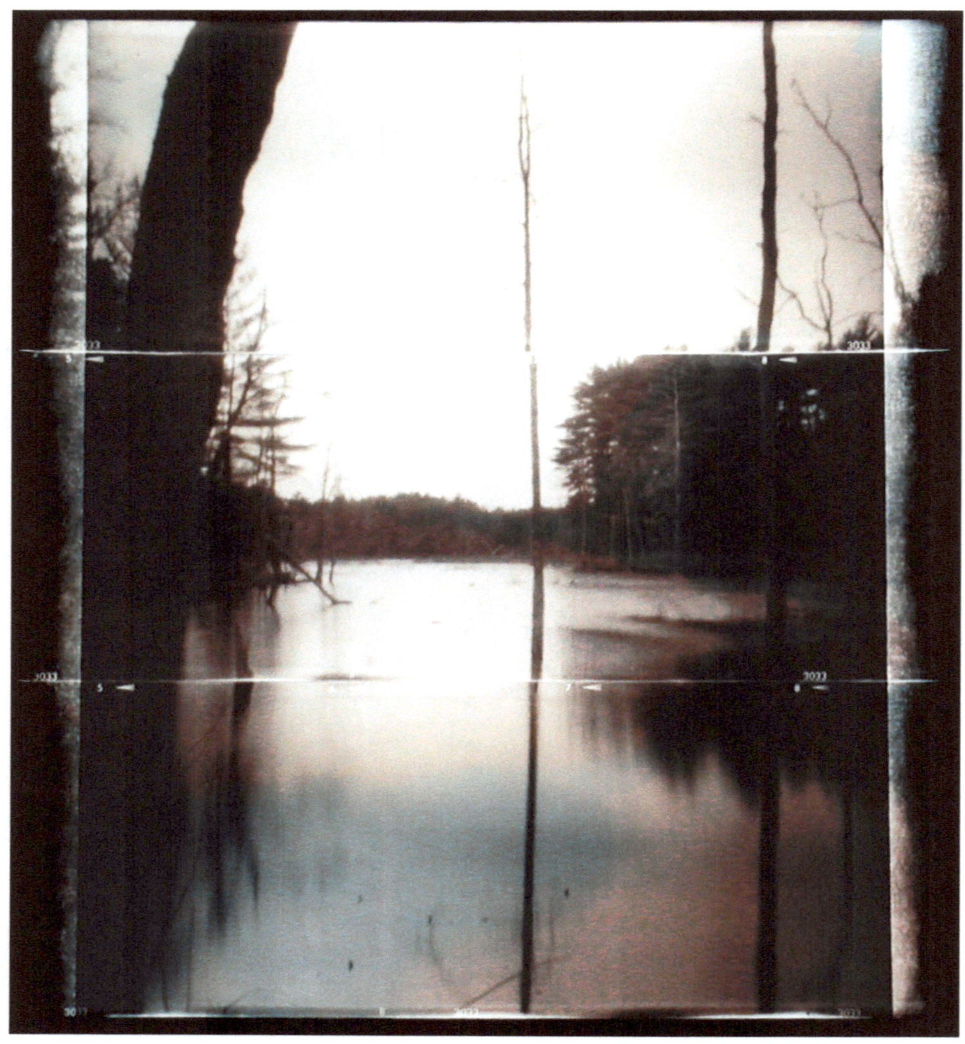

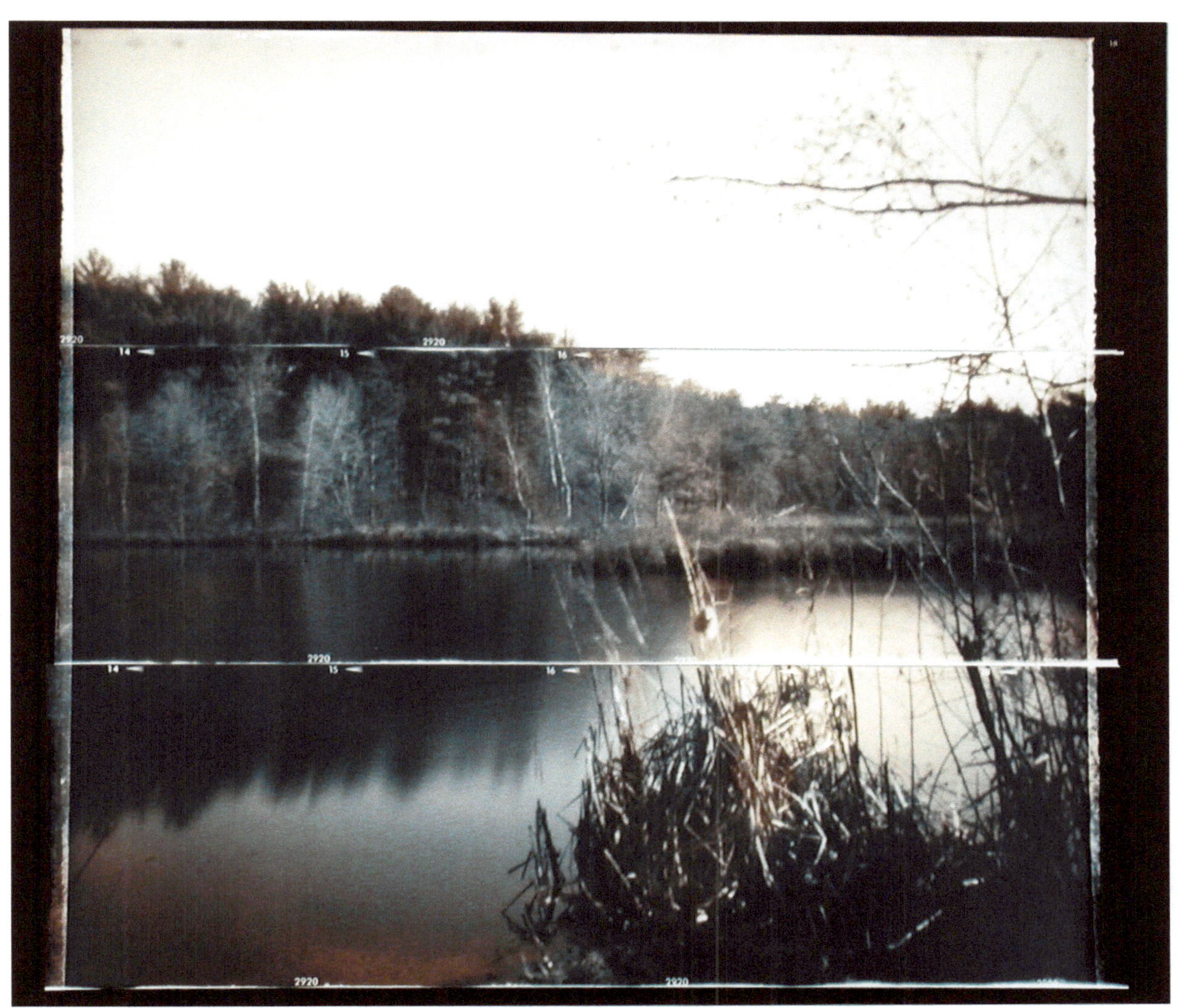

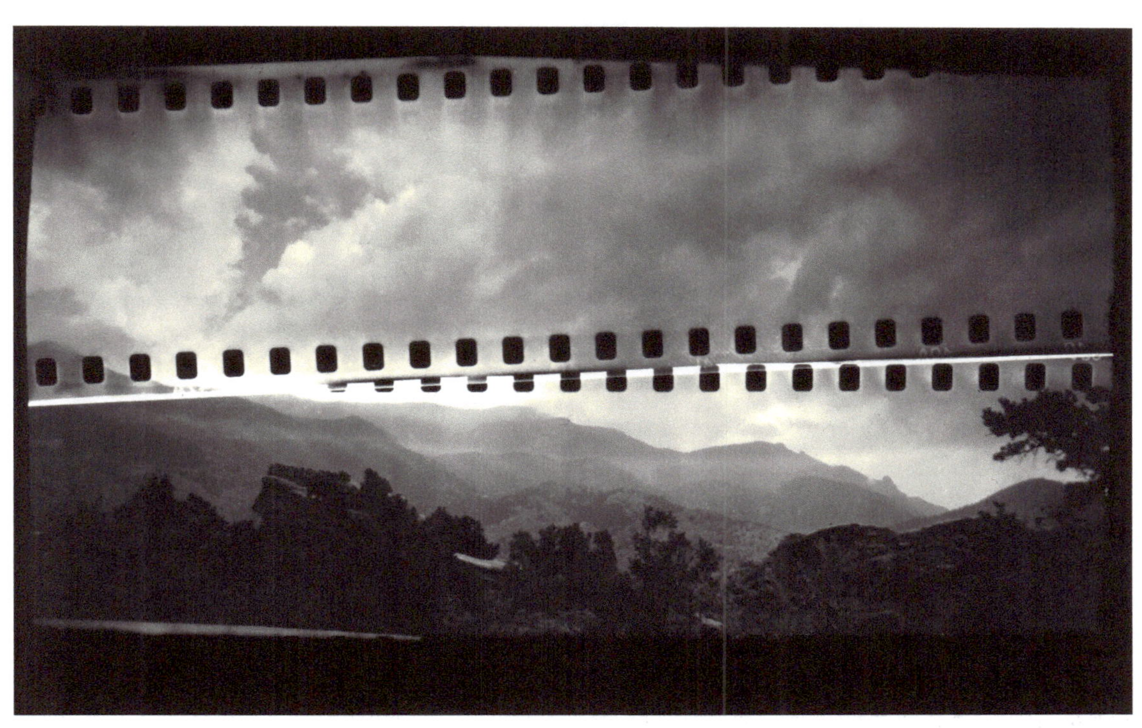

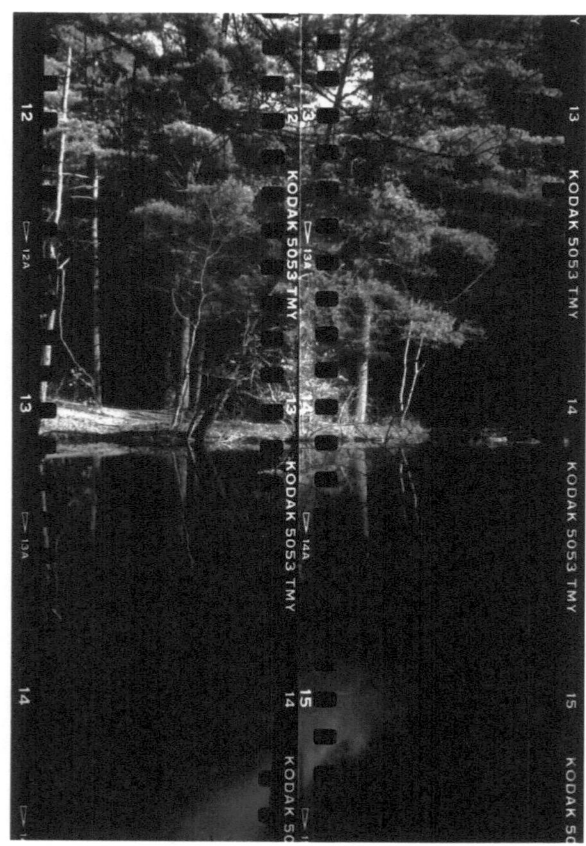
KODAK 5053 TMY

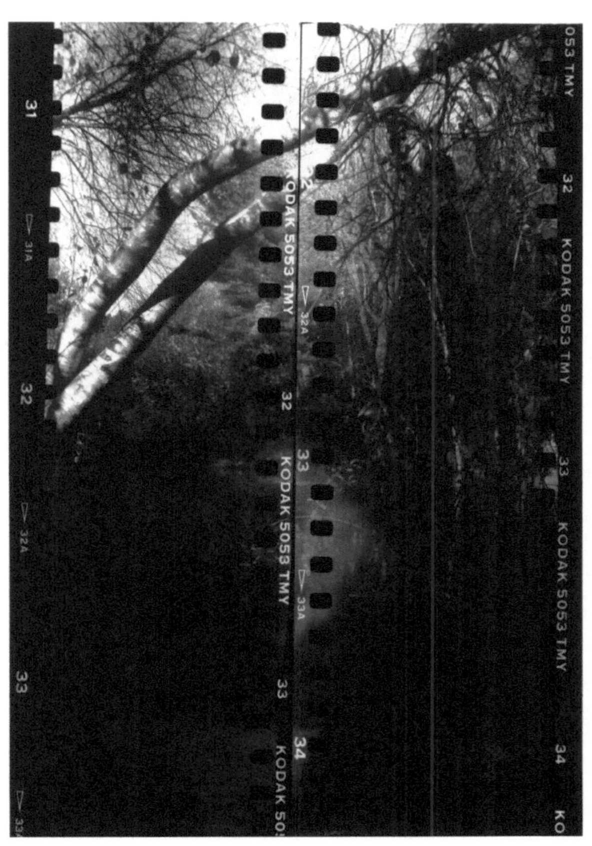
053 TMY
31
32
KODAK 5053 TMY
33
KODAK 5053 TMY
34

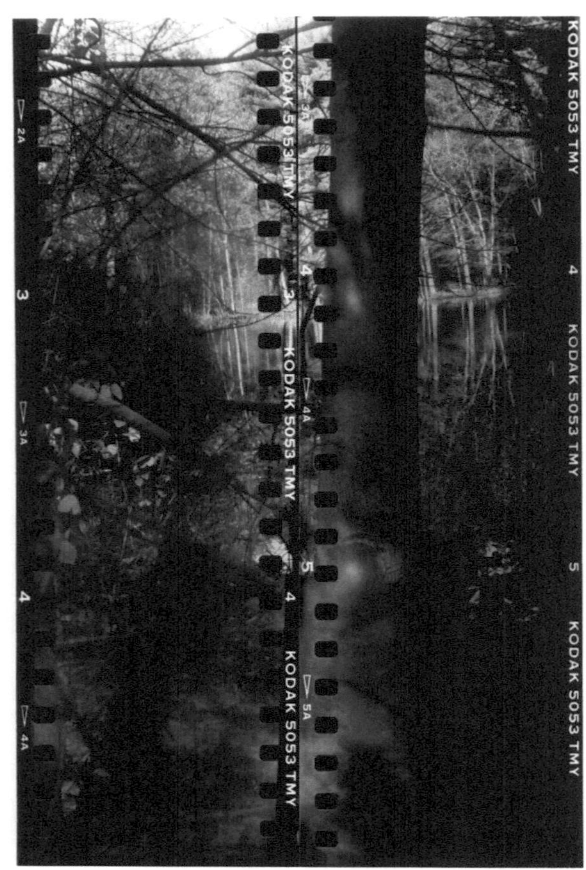
KODAK 5053 TMY
KODAK 5053 TMY
KODAK 5053 TMY
KODAK 5053 TMY
KODAK 5053 TMY
KODAK 5053 TMY
KODAK 5053 TMY

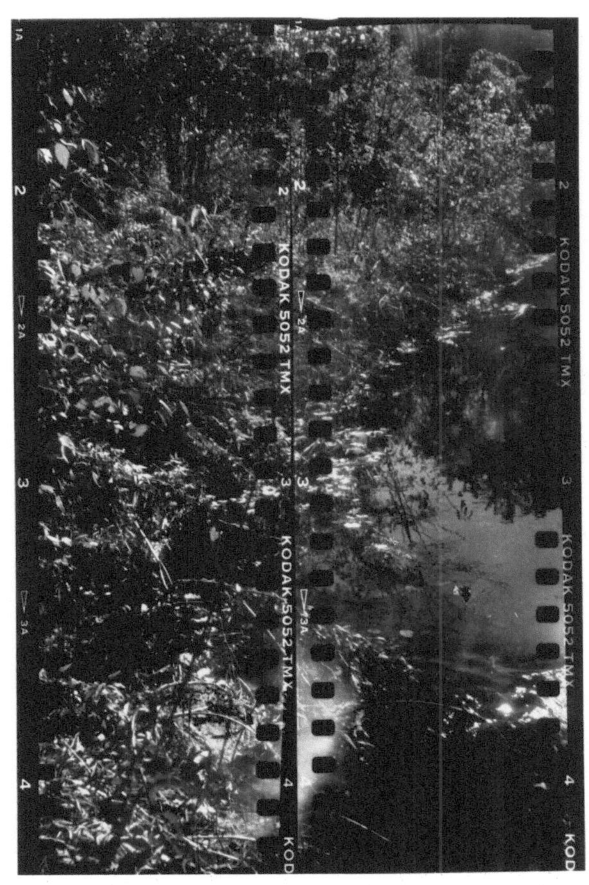
KODAK 5052 TMX
KODAK 5052 TMX

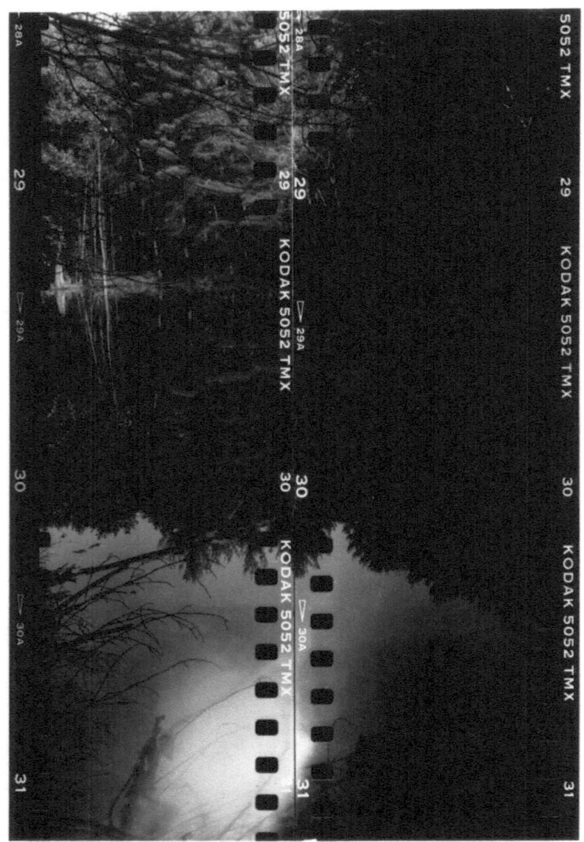
5052 TMX
29
KODAK 5052 TMX
30
KODAK 5052 TMX
31

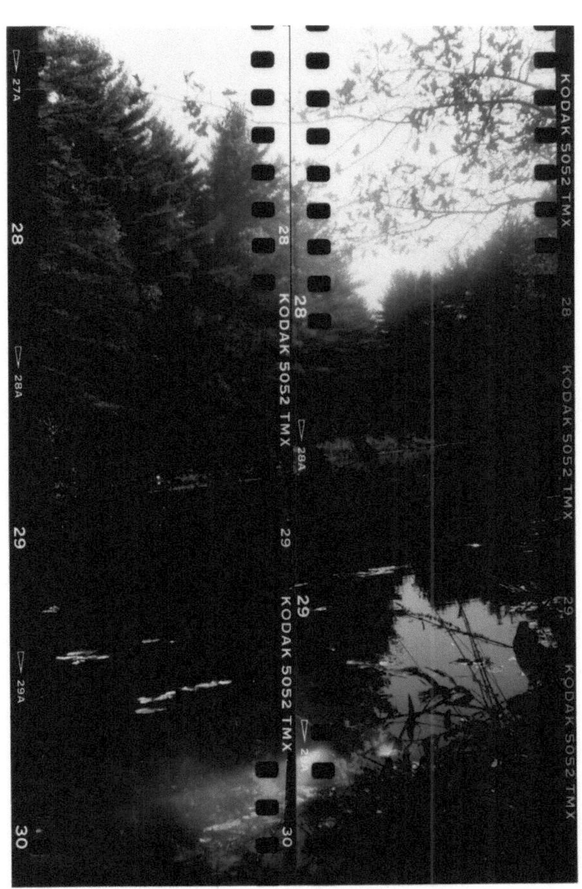
KODAK 5052 TMX

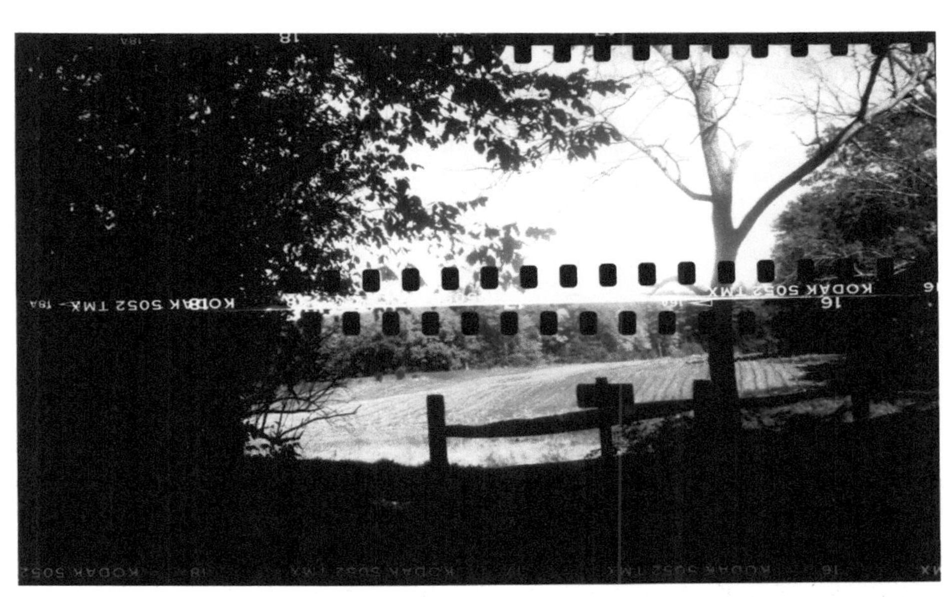

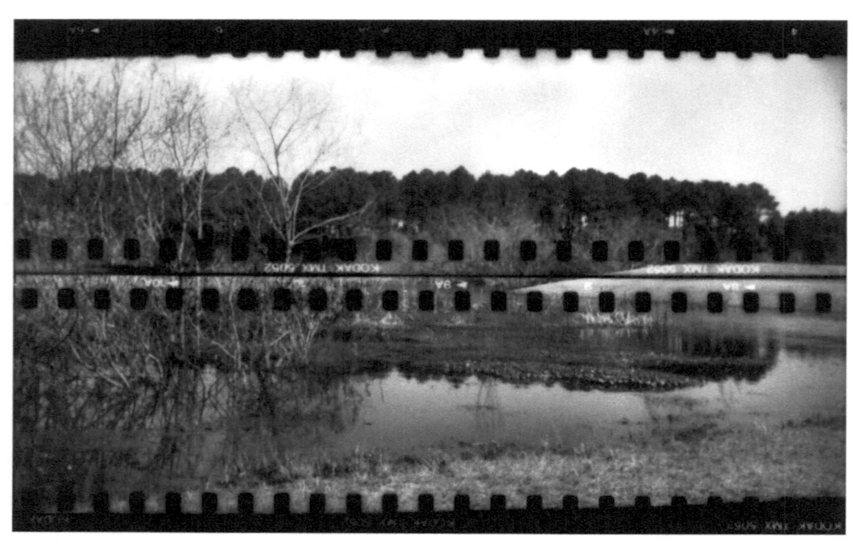

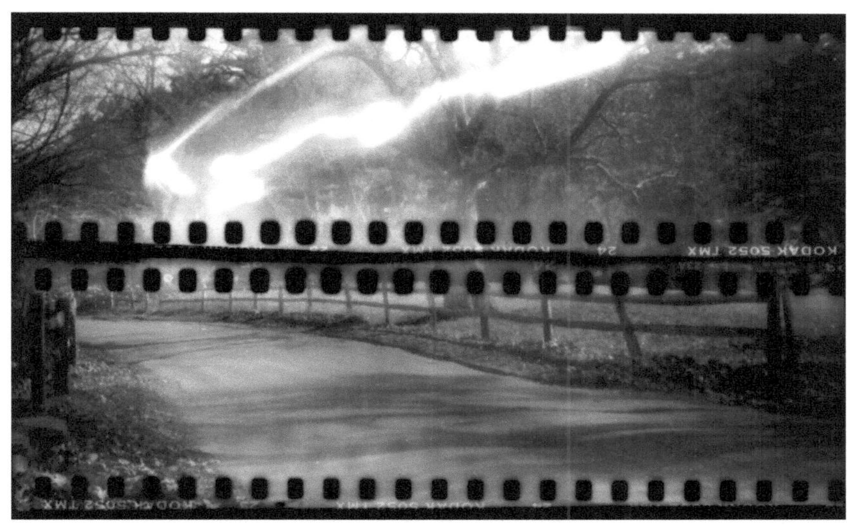
KODAK 5052 TMX

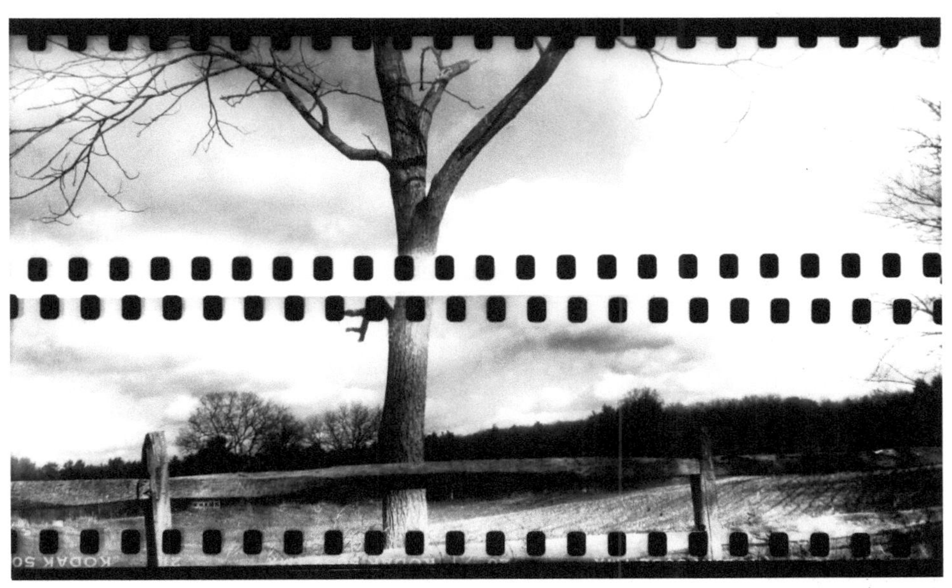

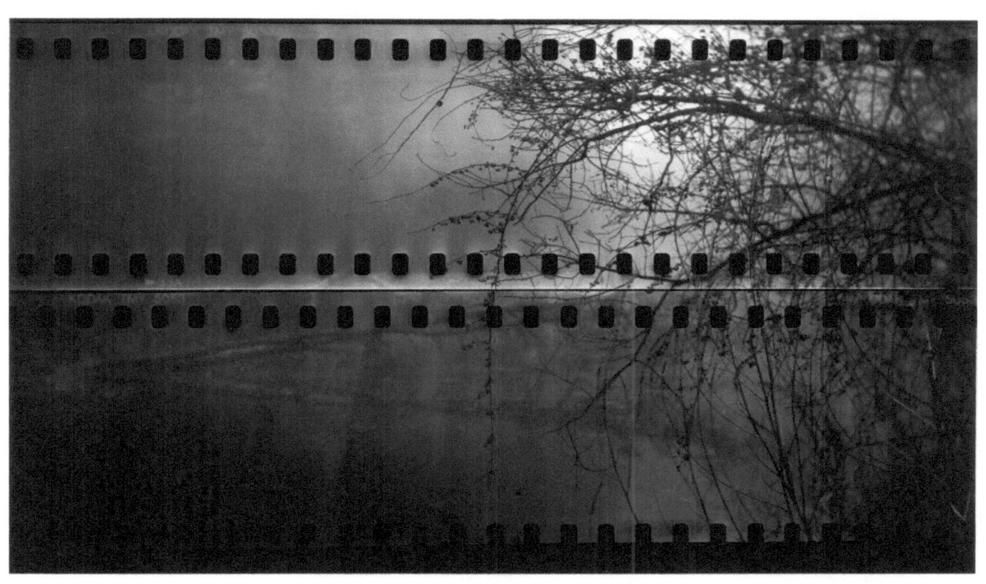

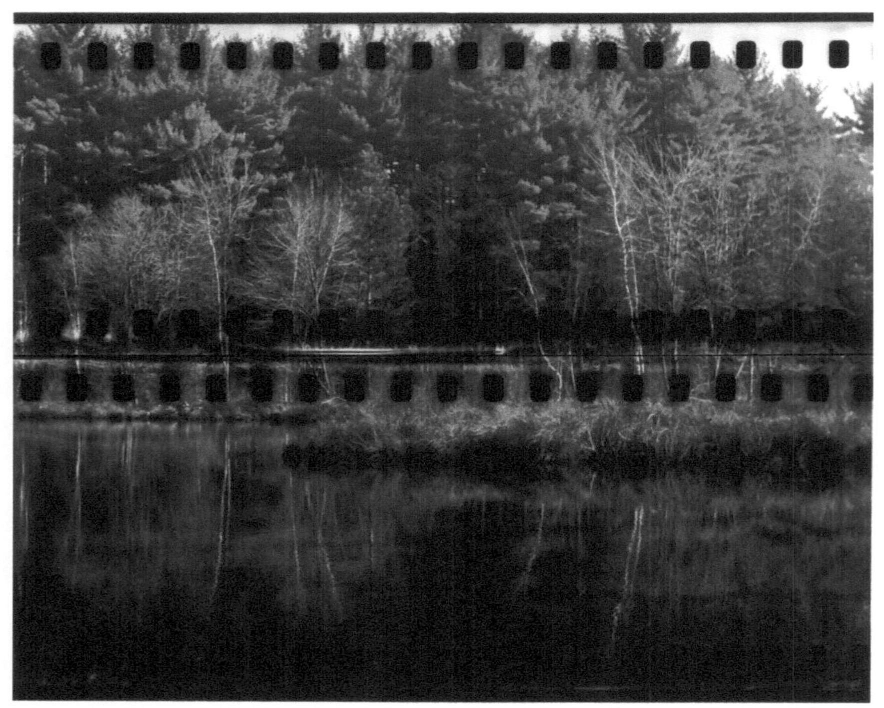

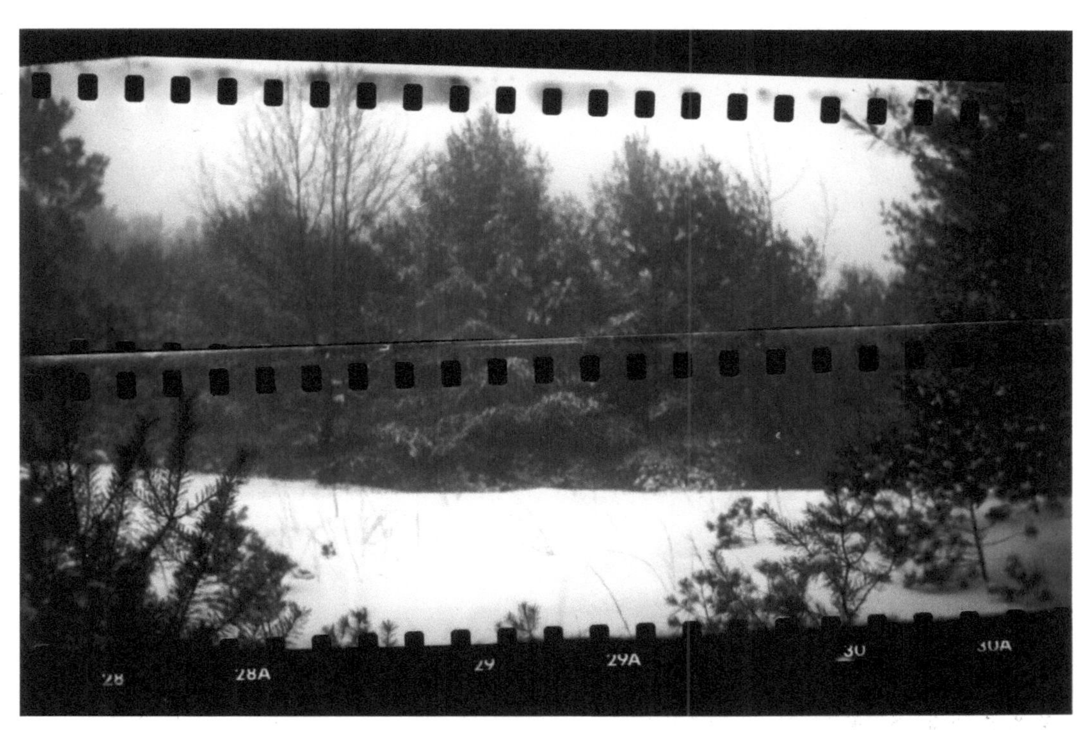
28
28A
29
29A
30
30A

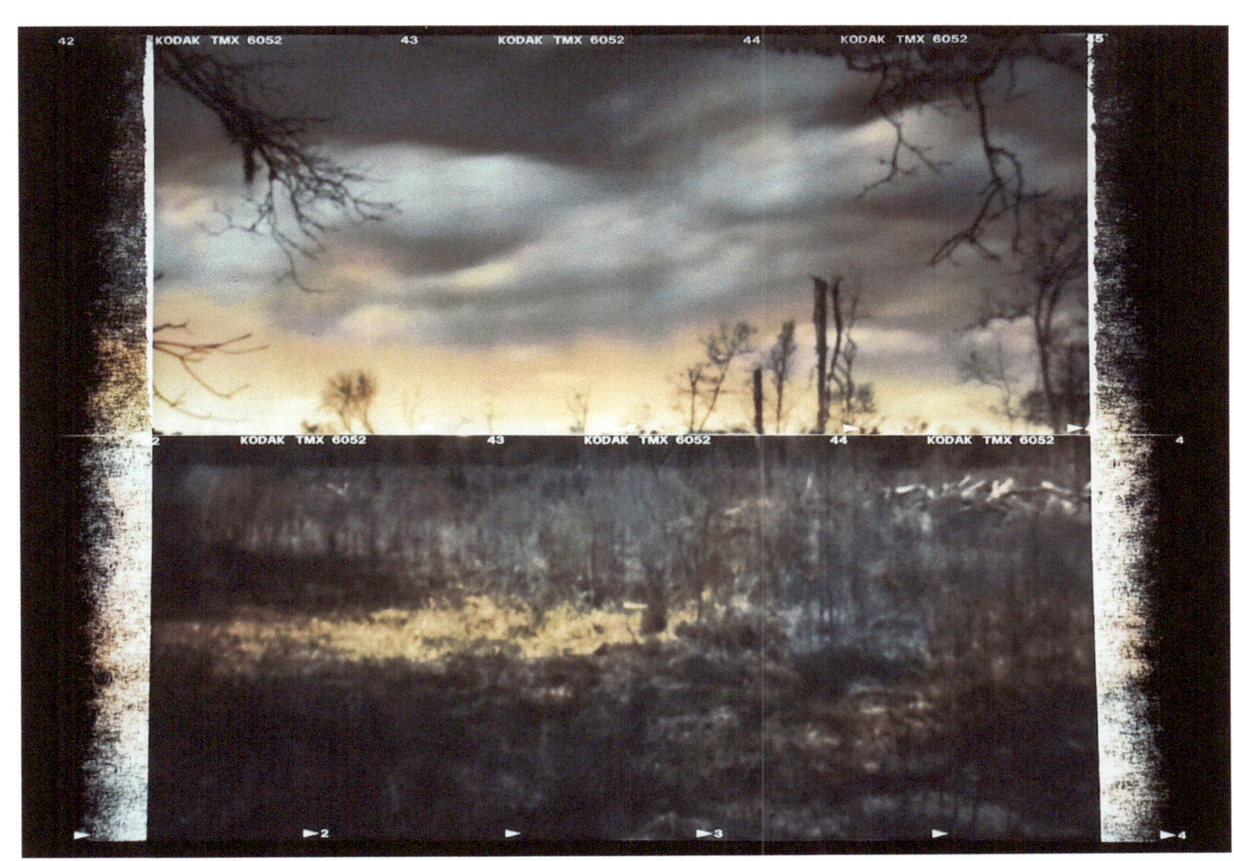
42
KODAK TMX 6052
43
KODAK TMX 6052
44
KODAK TMX 6052
KODAK TMX 6052
43
KODAK TMX 6052
44
KODAK TMX 6052
4
2
3
4

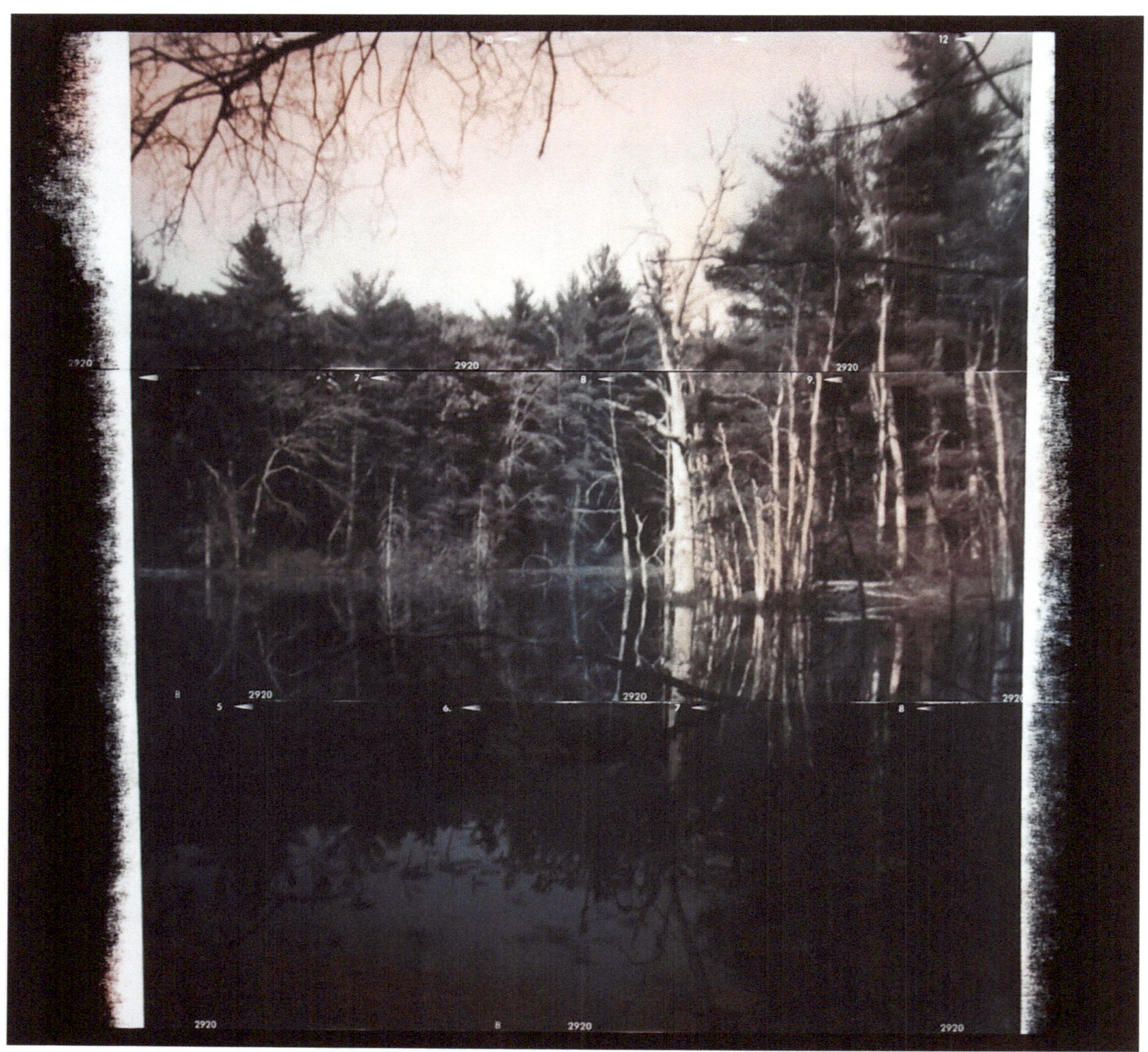

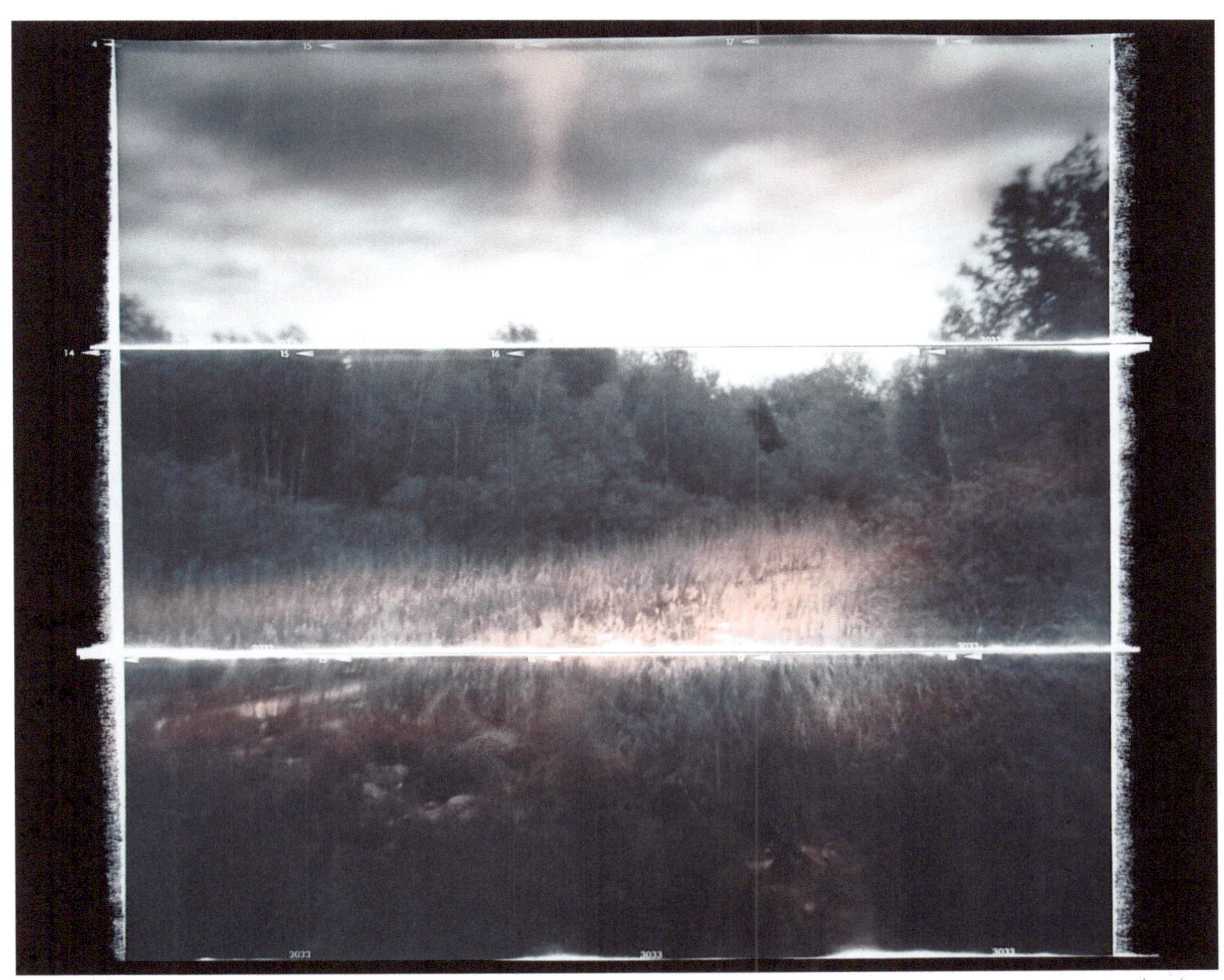

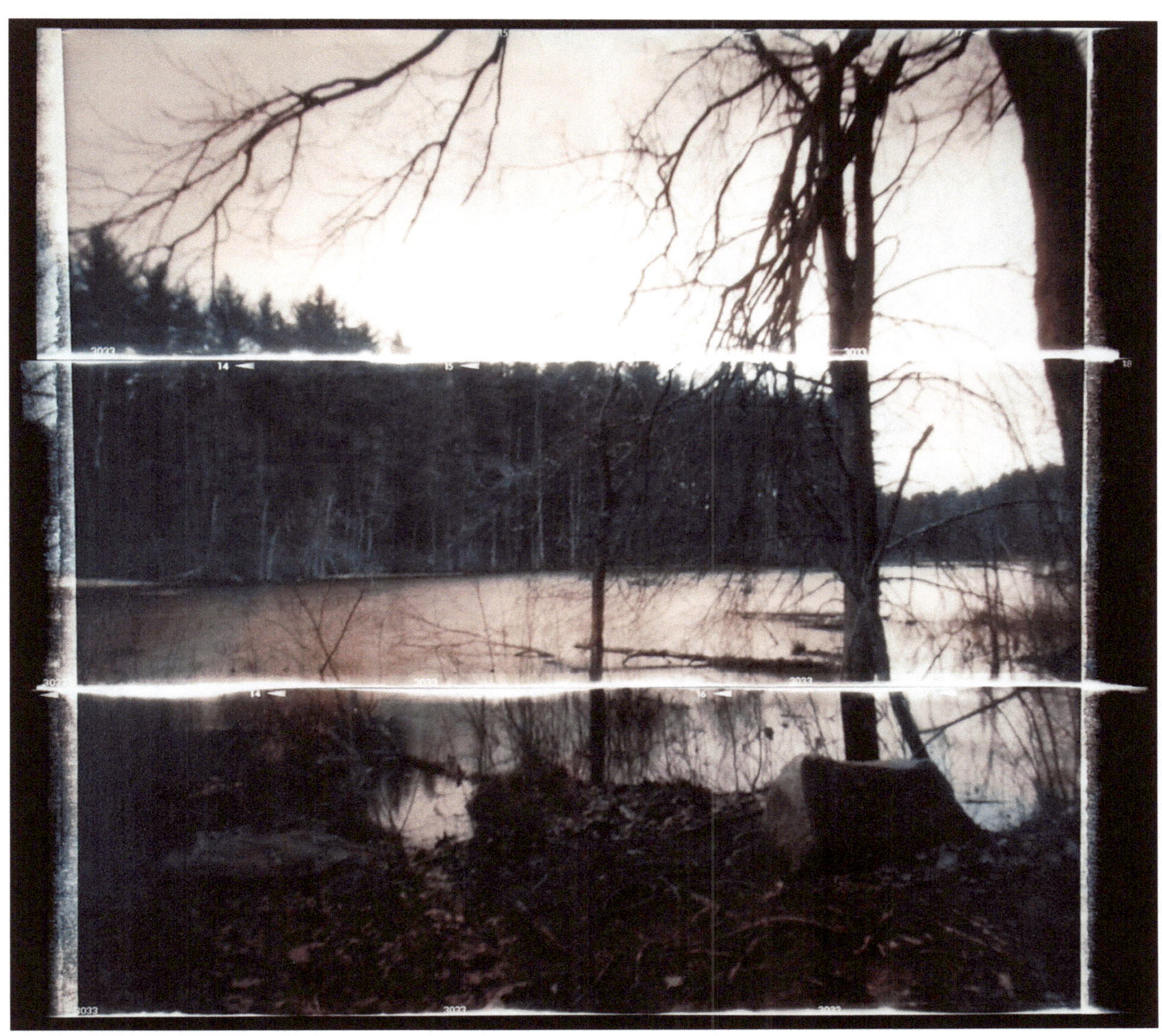

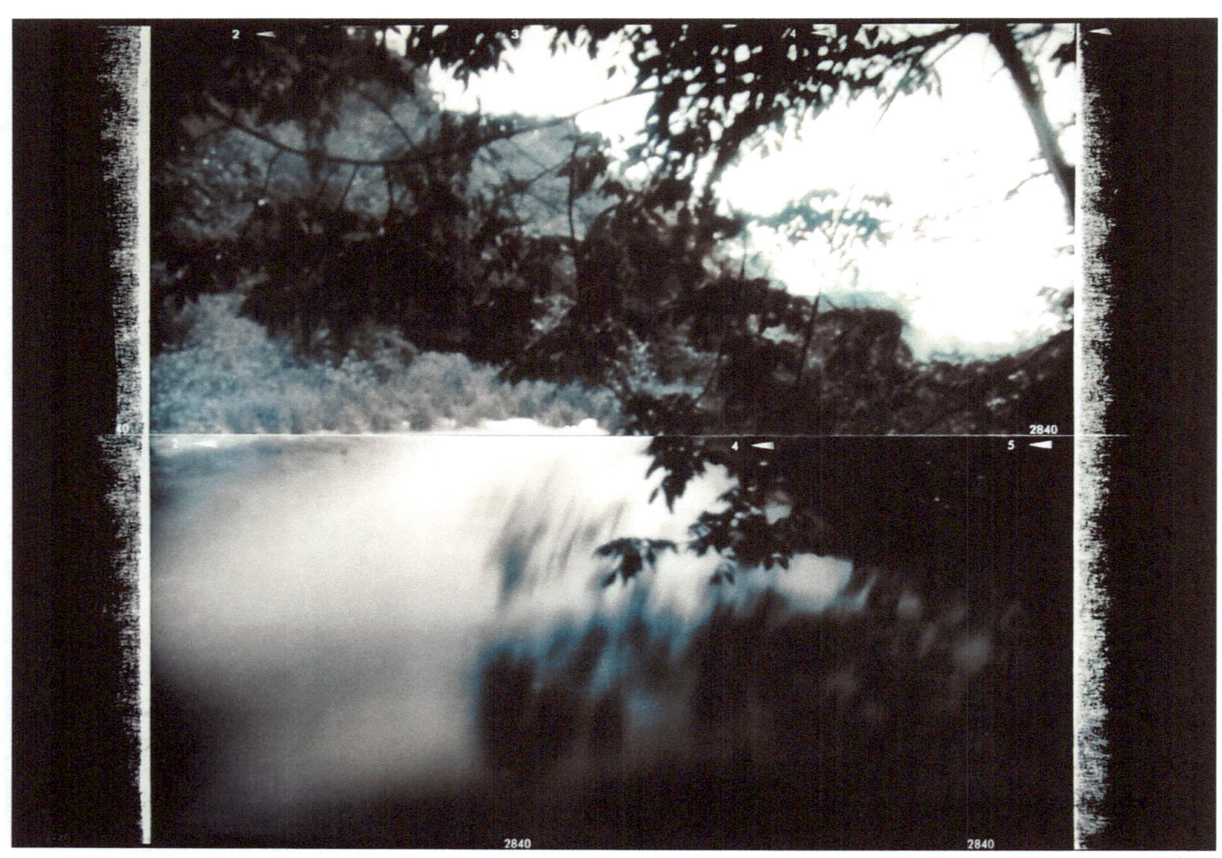

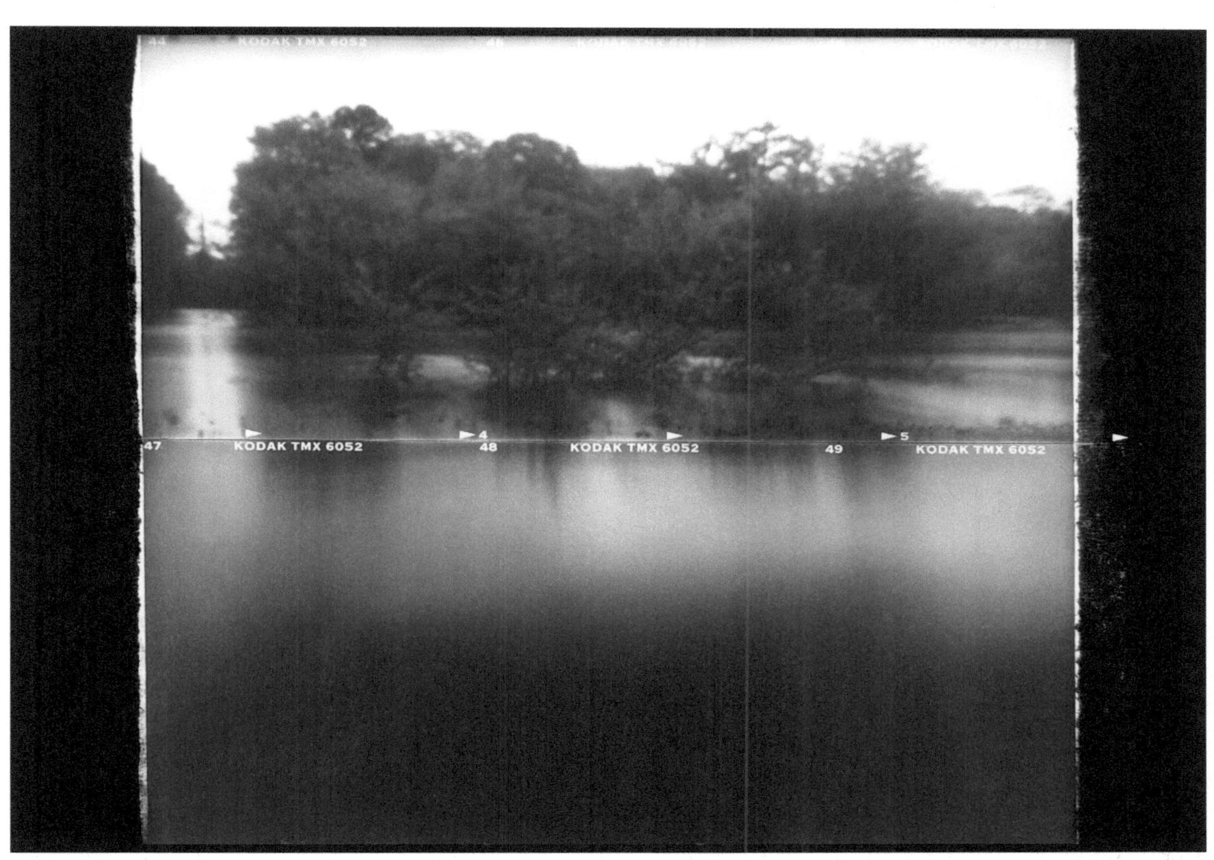
KODAK TMX 6052
4
5
47
KODAK TMX 6052
48
KODAK TMX 6052
49
KODAK TMX 6052

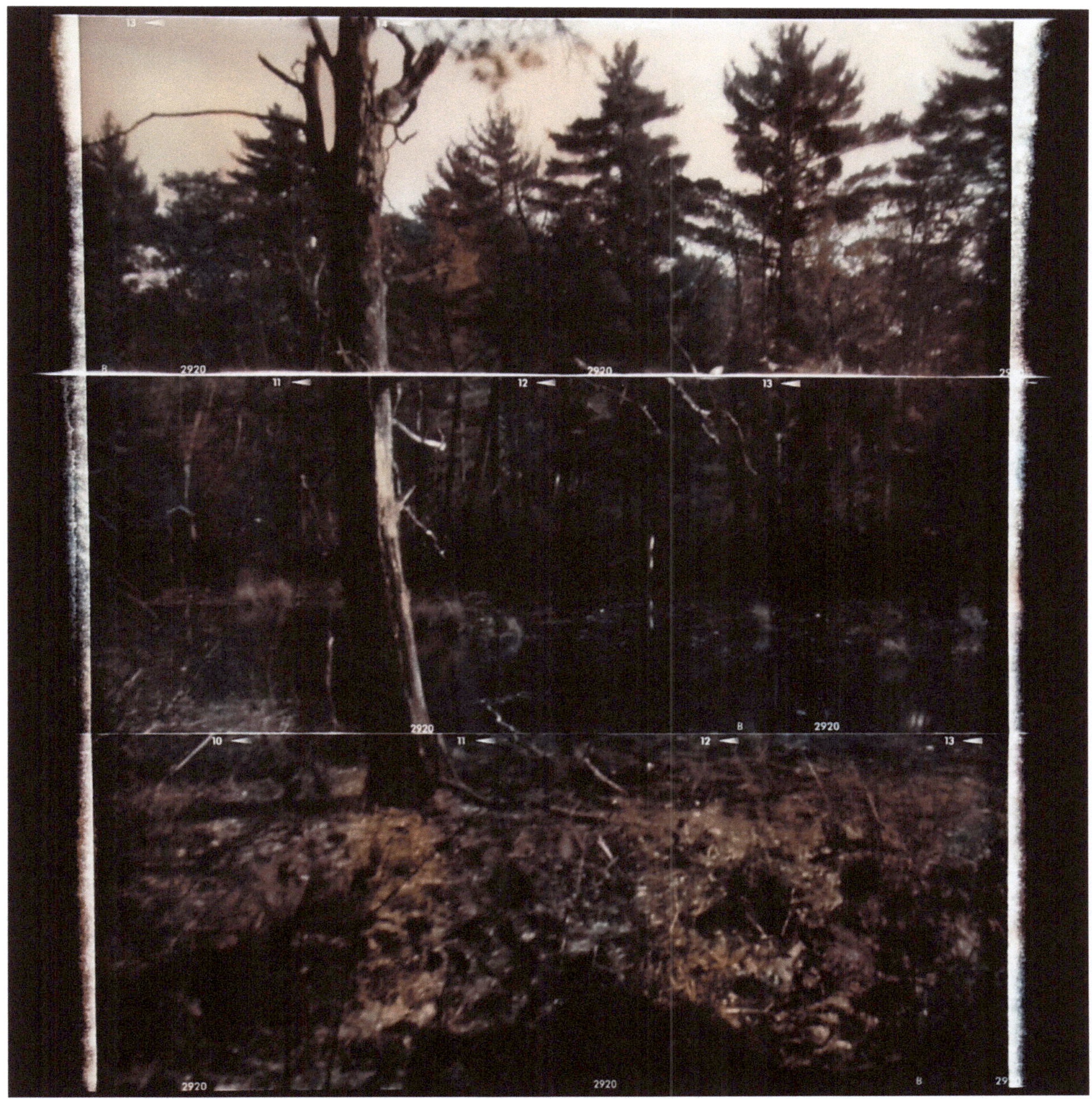

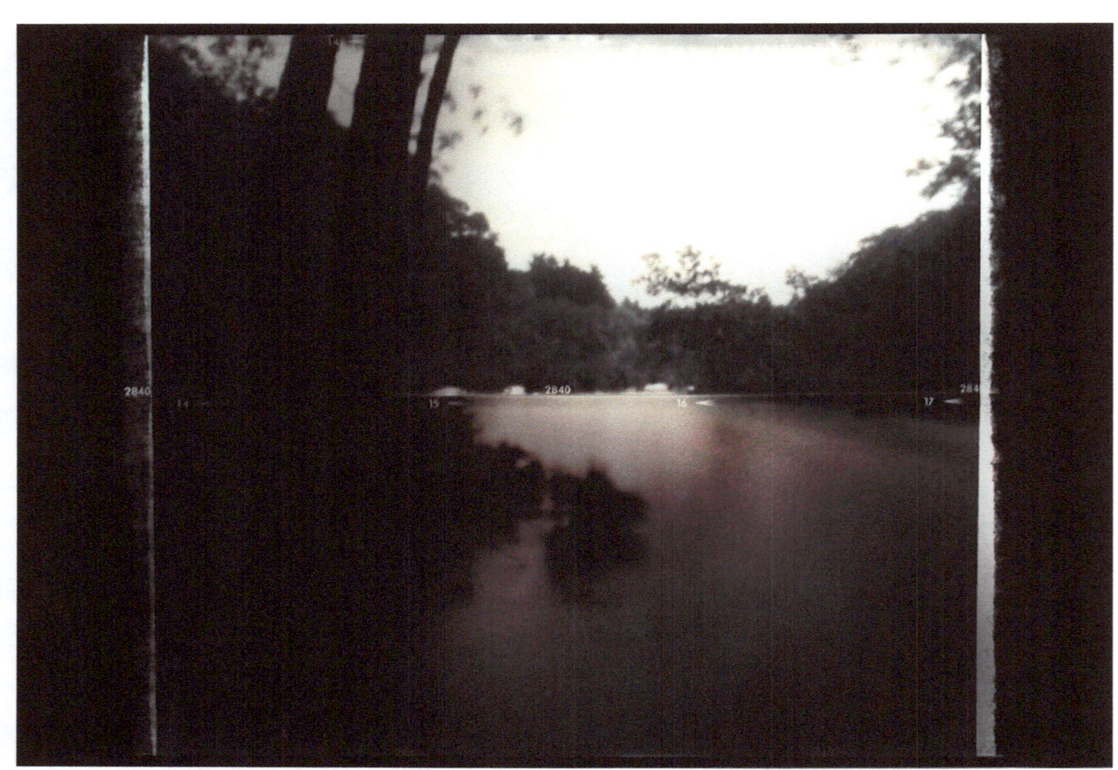
2840
2840
15
16
17

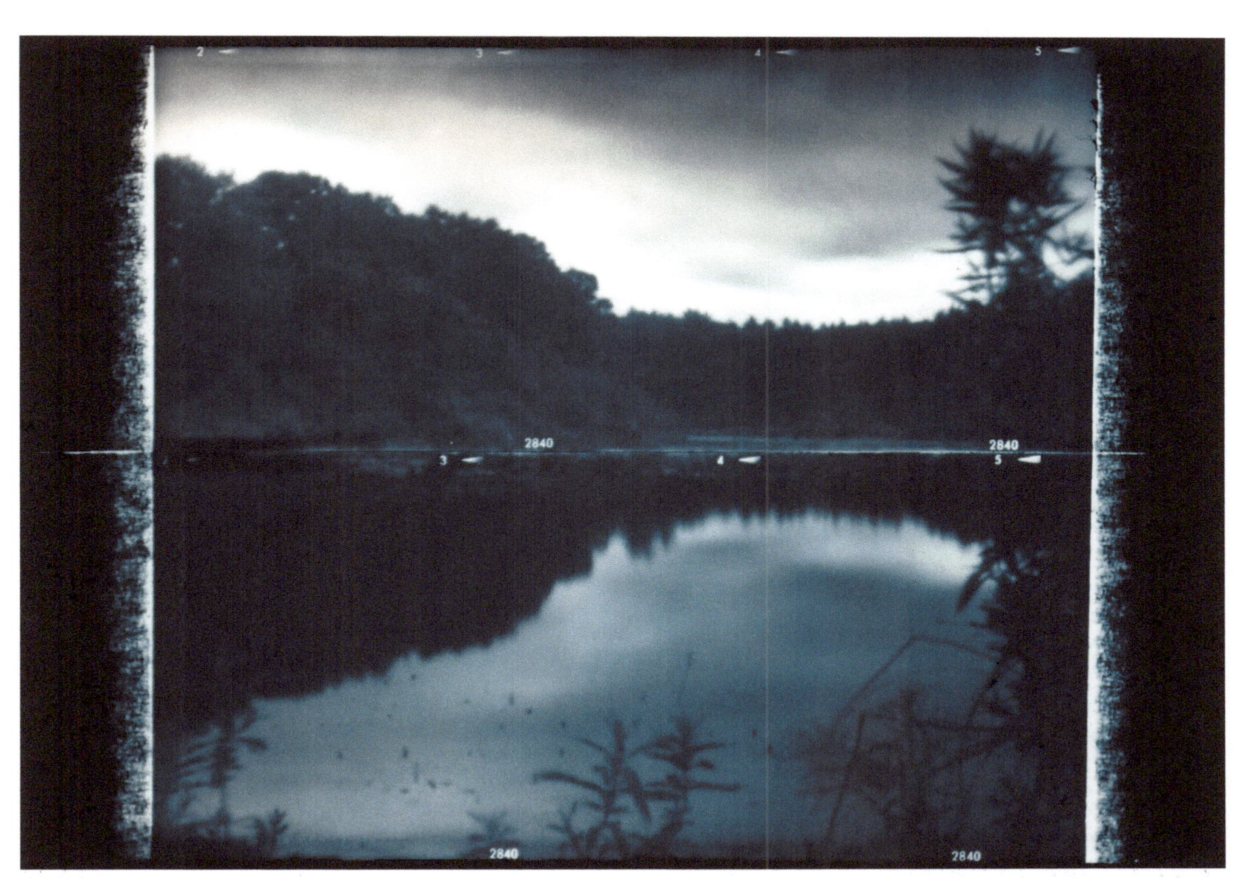

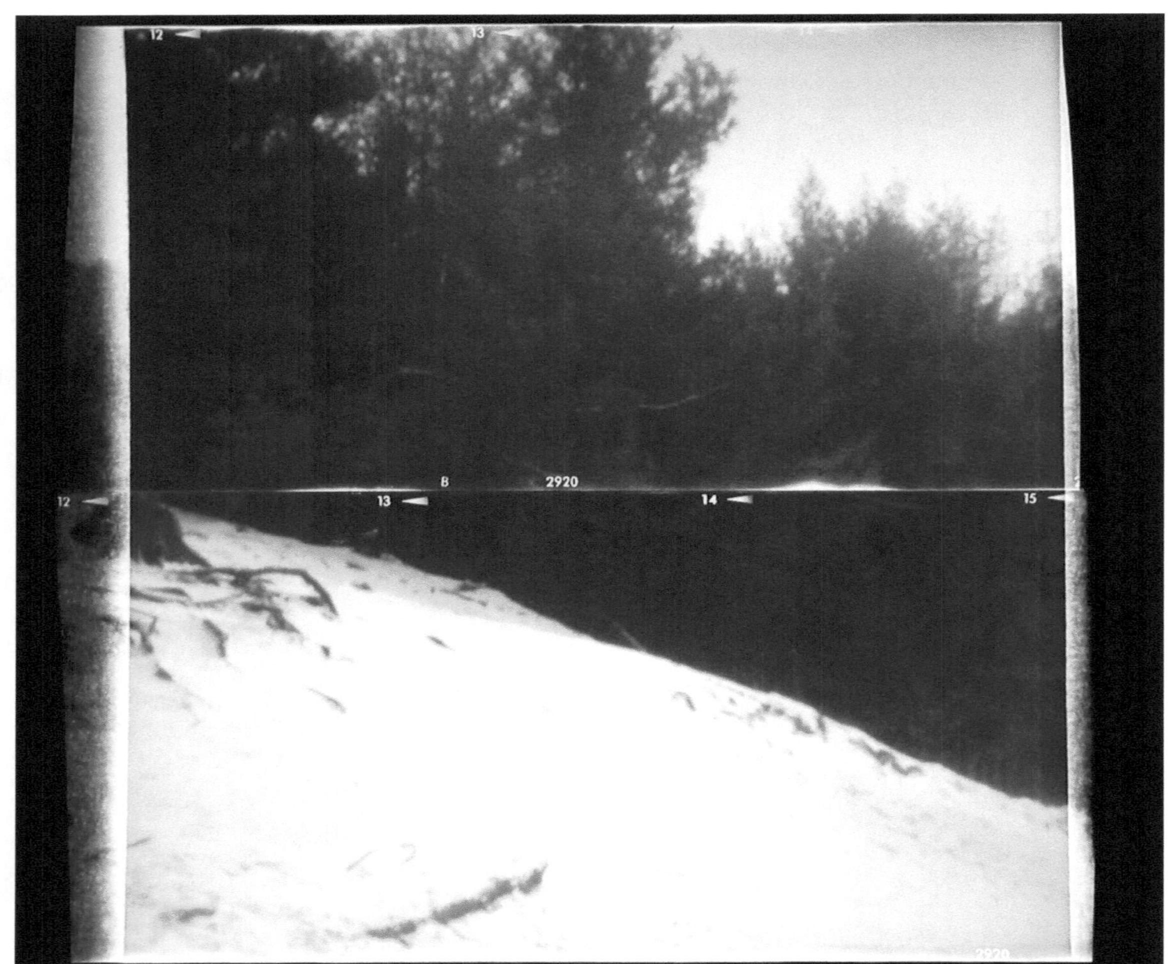
12
13
B
2920
12
13
14
15

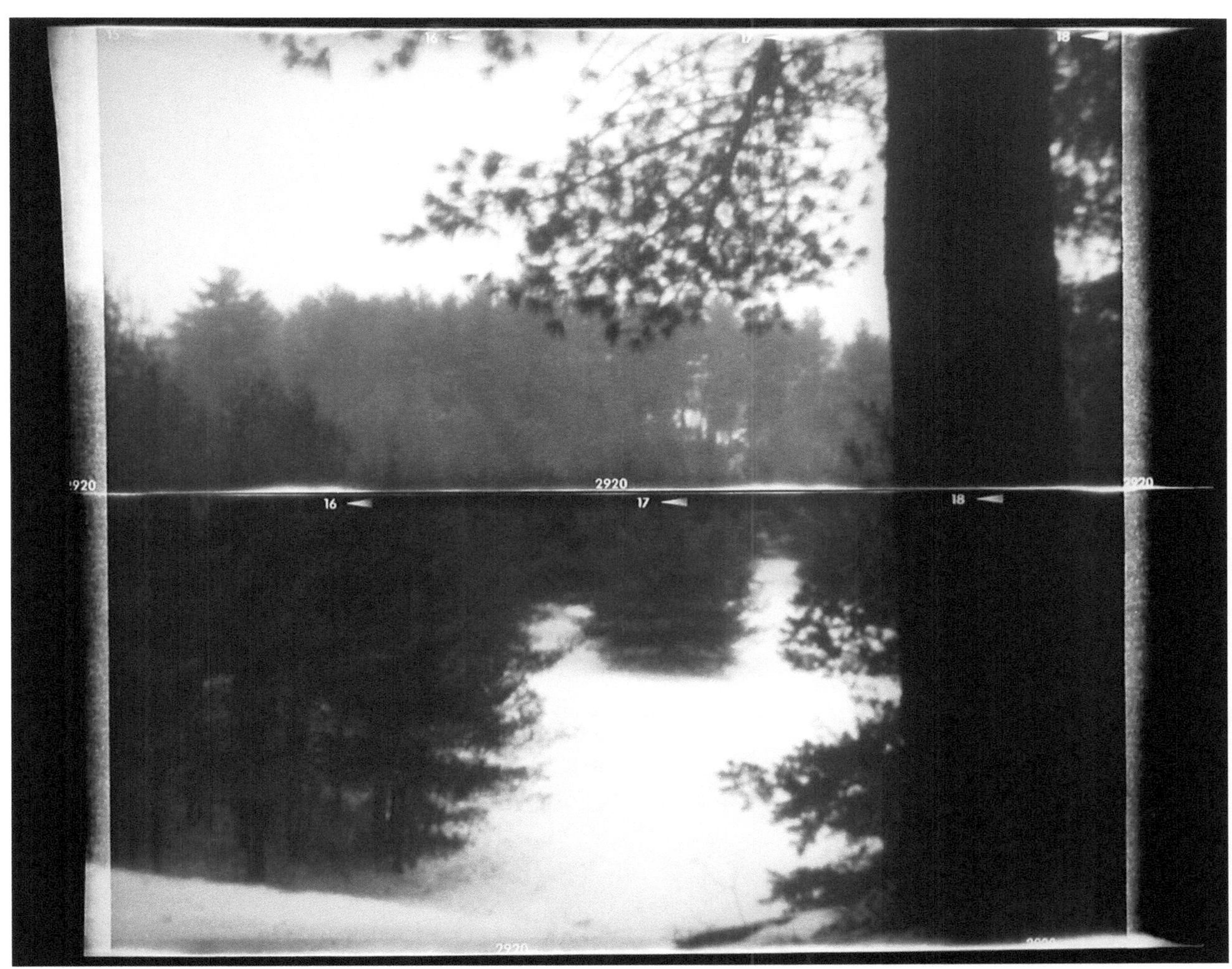
2920
16
17
18
2920
2920

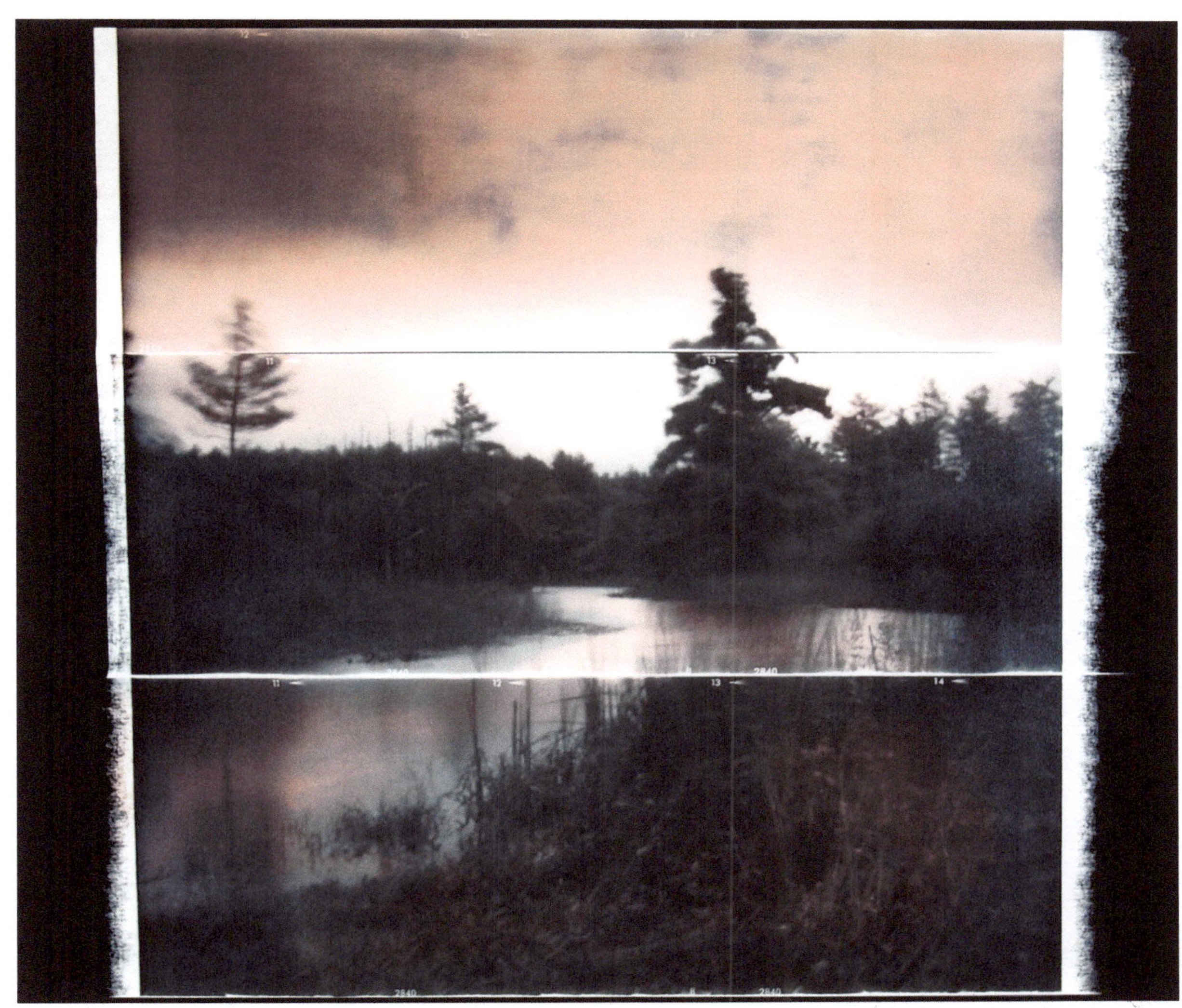

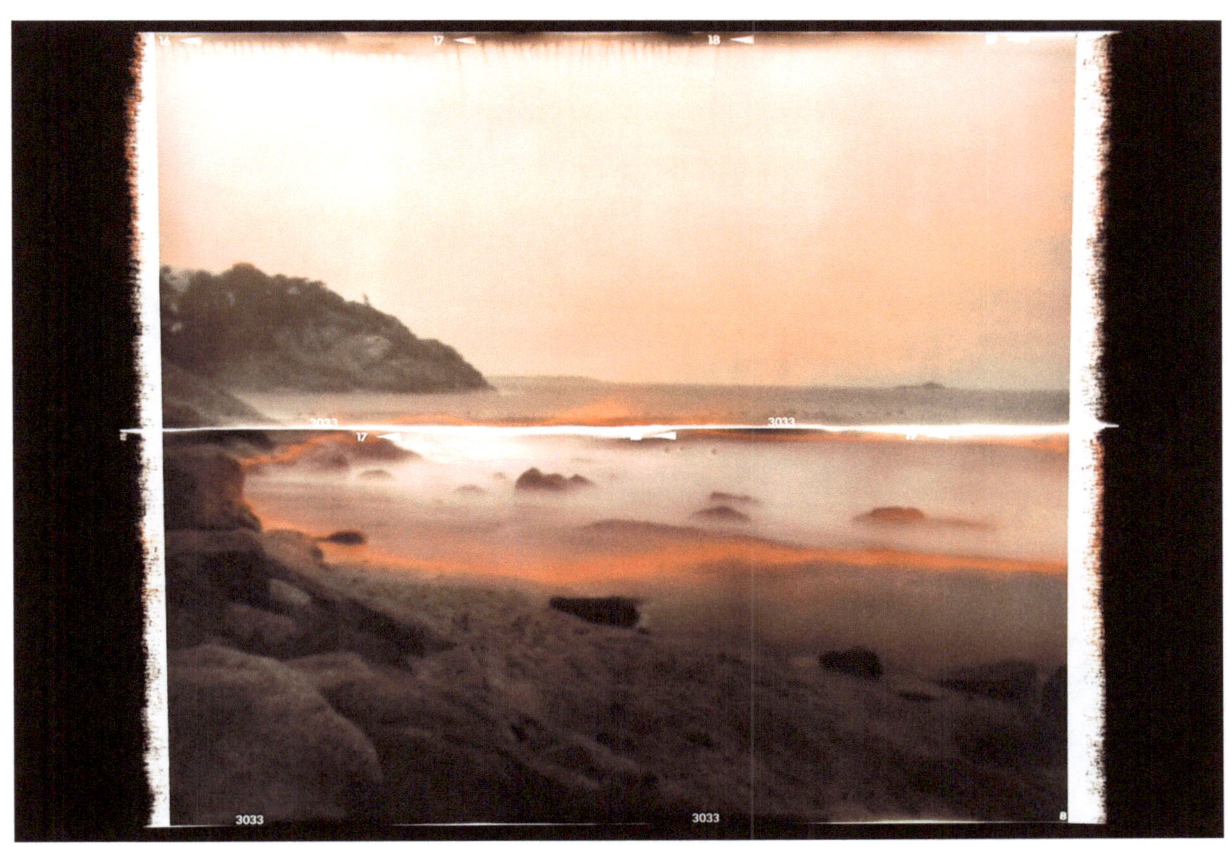

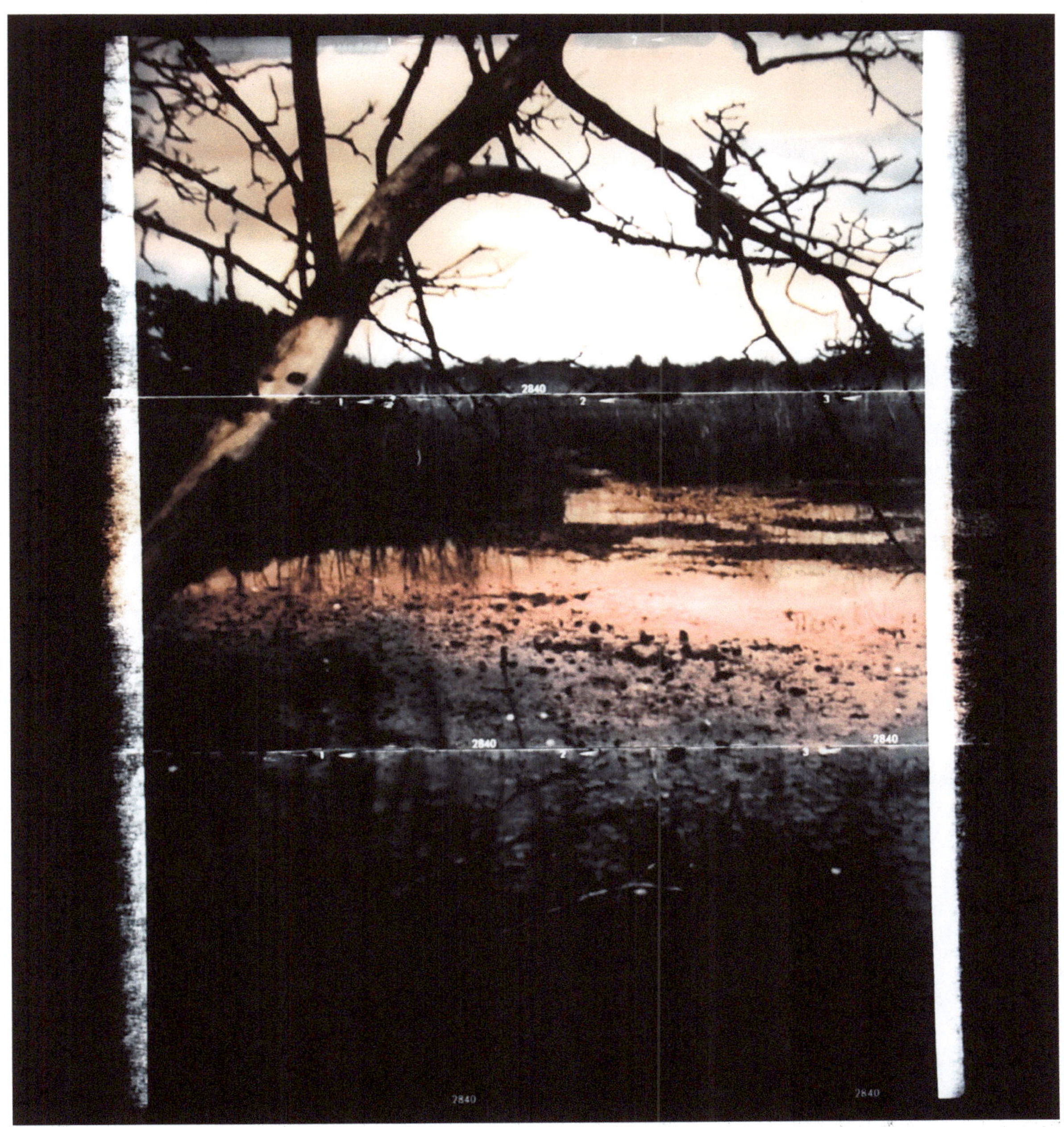
2840
2840
2840
2840
2840

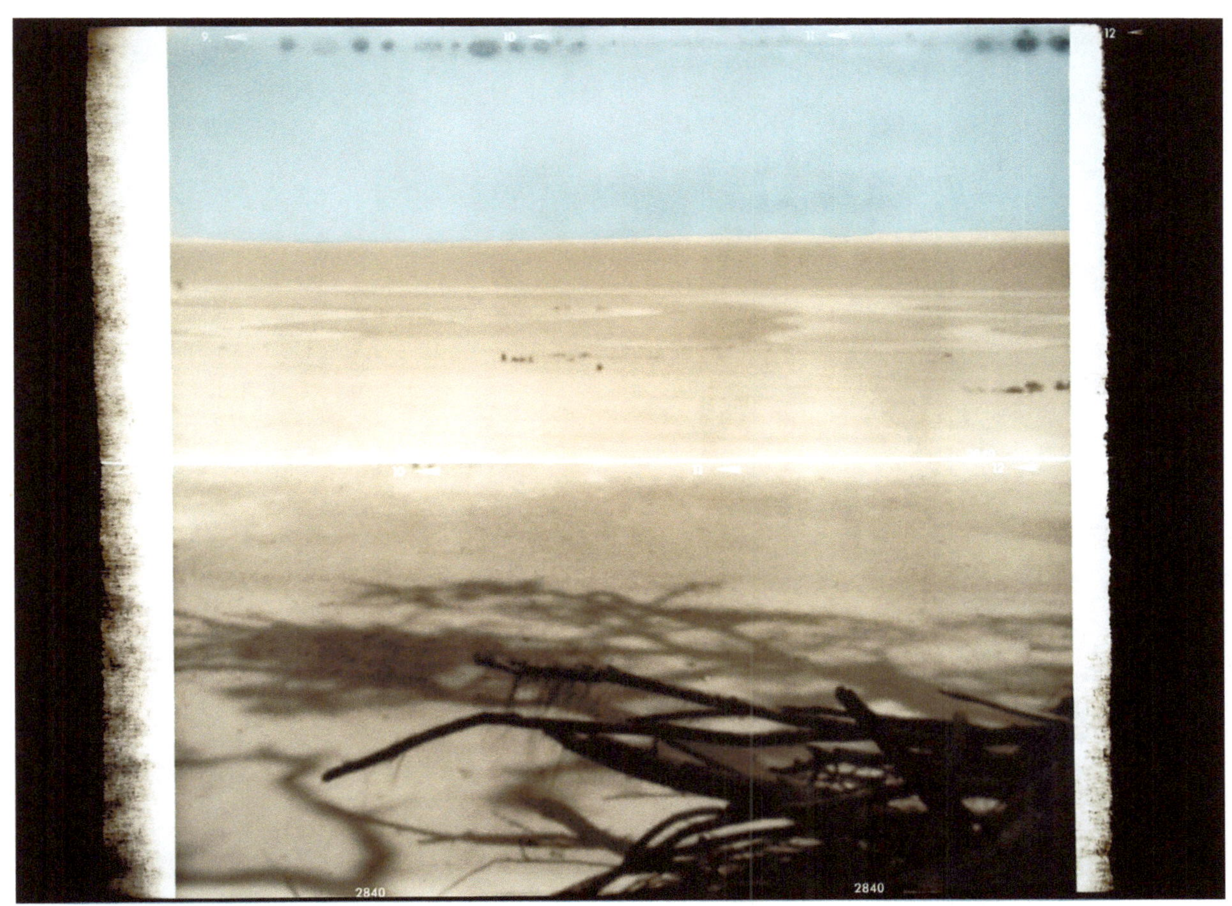
2840
2840

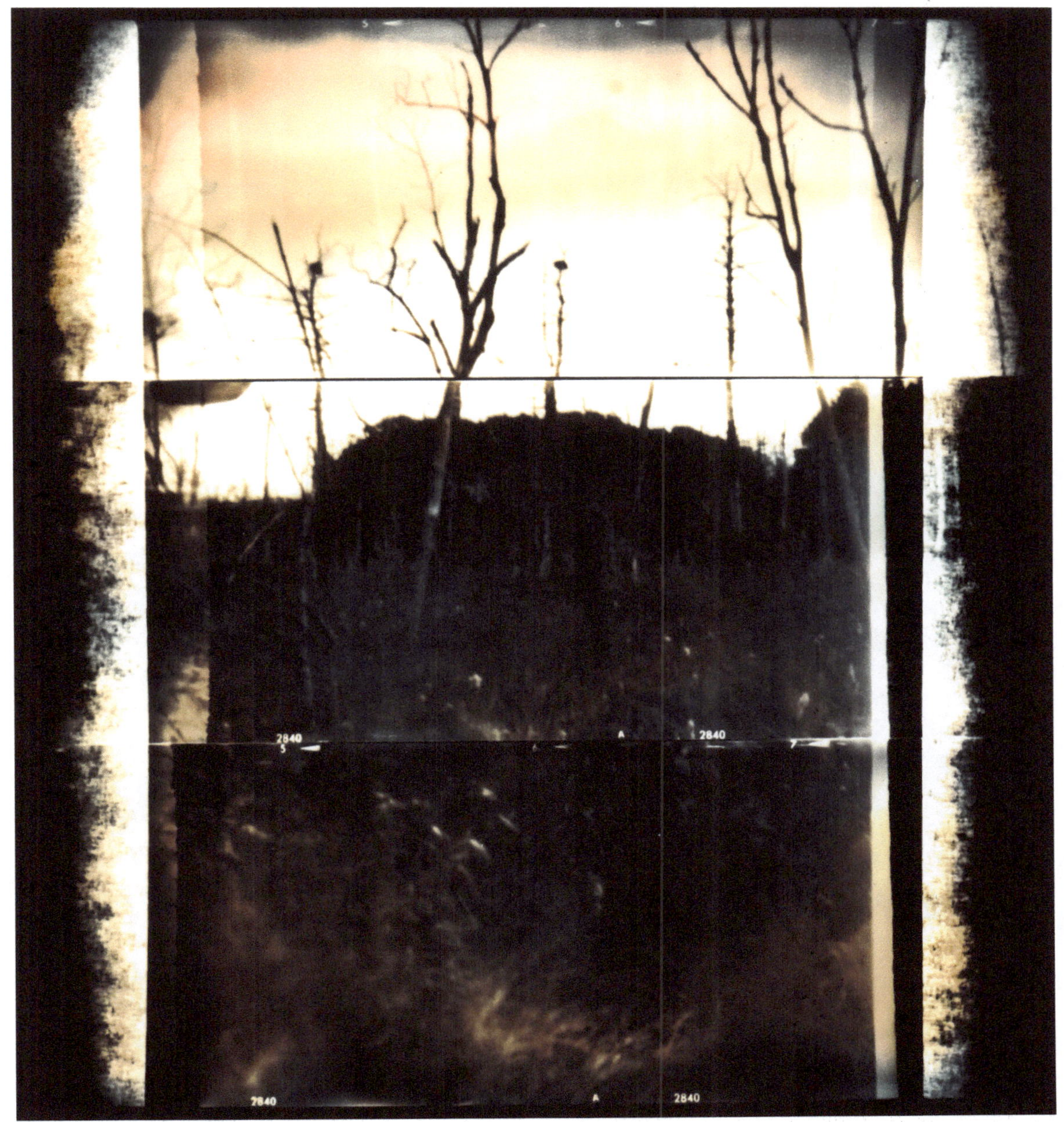

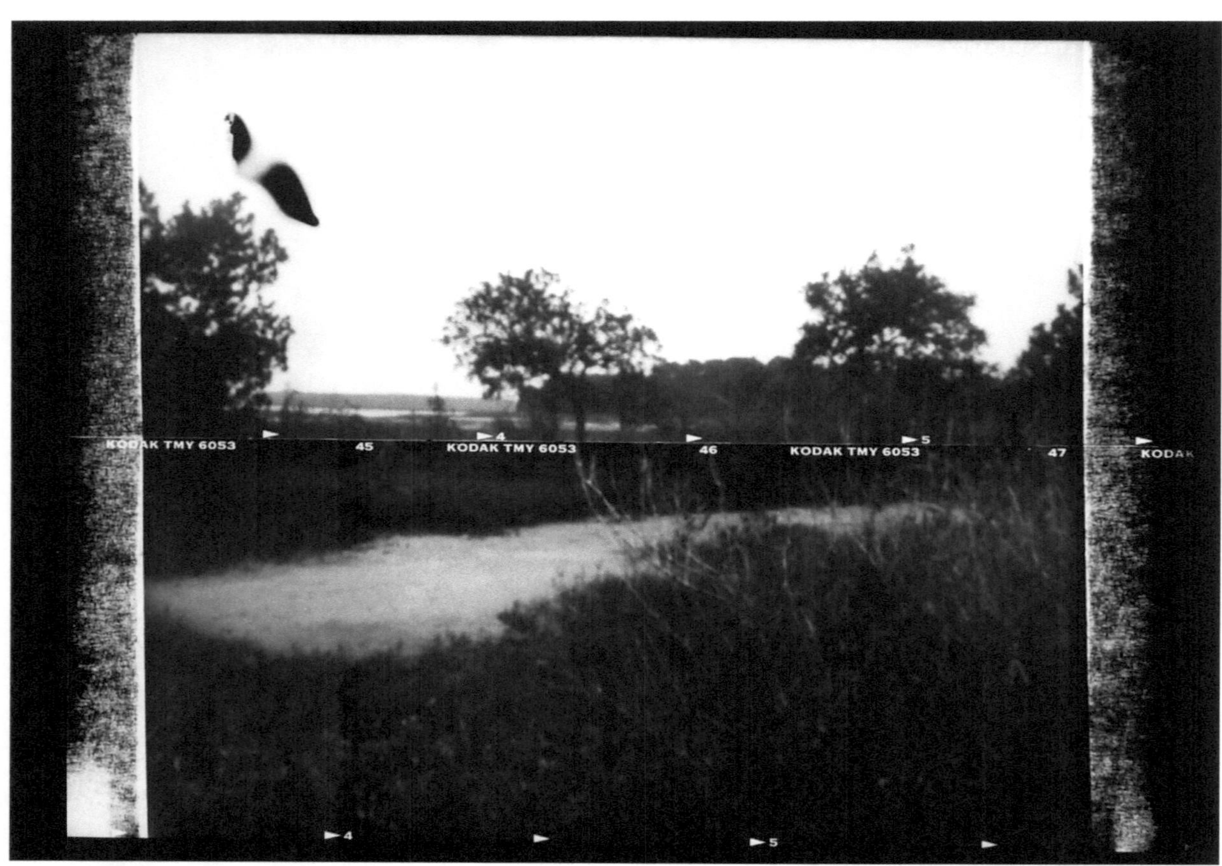
KODAK TMY 6053
45
KODAK TMY 6053
46
KODAK TMY 6053
47
KODAK

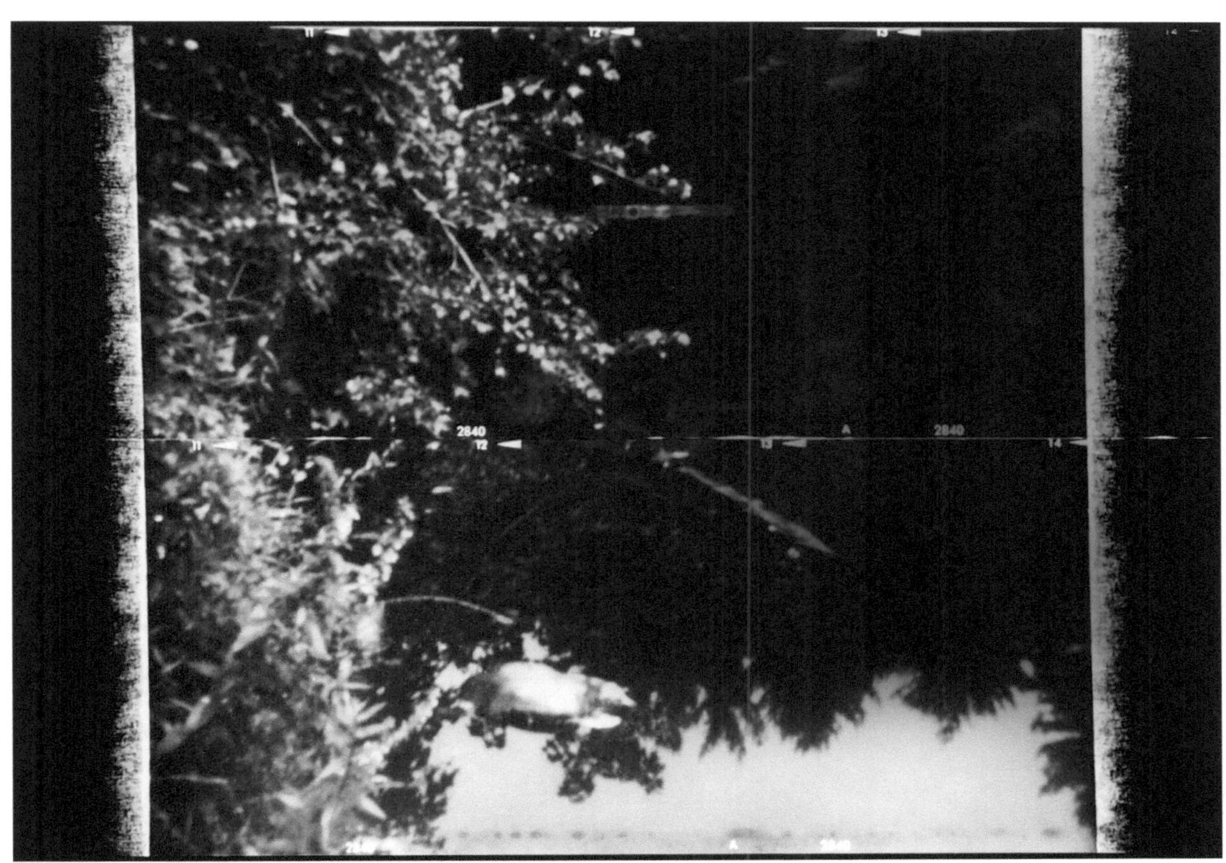

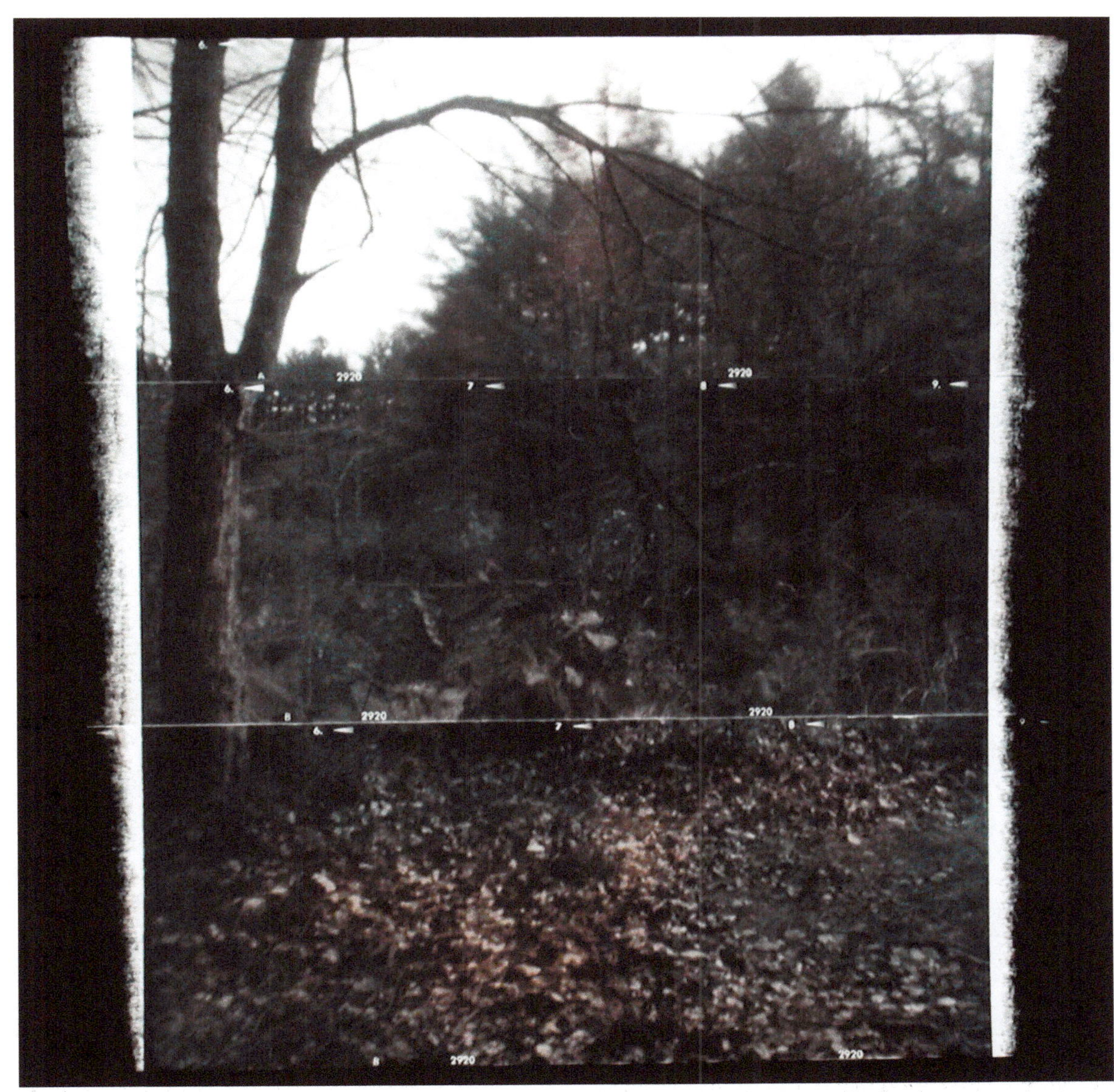

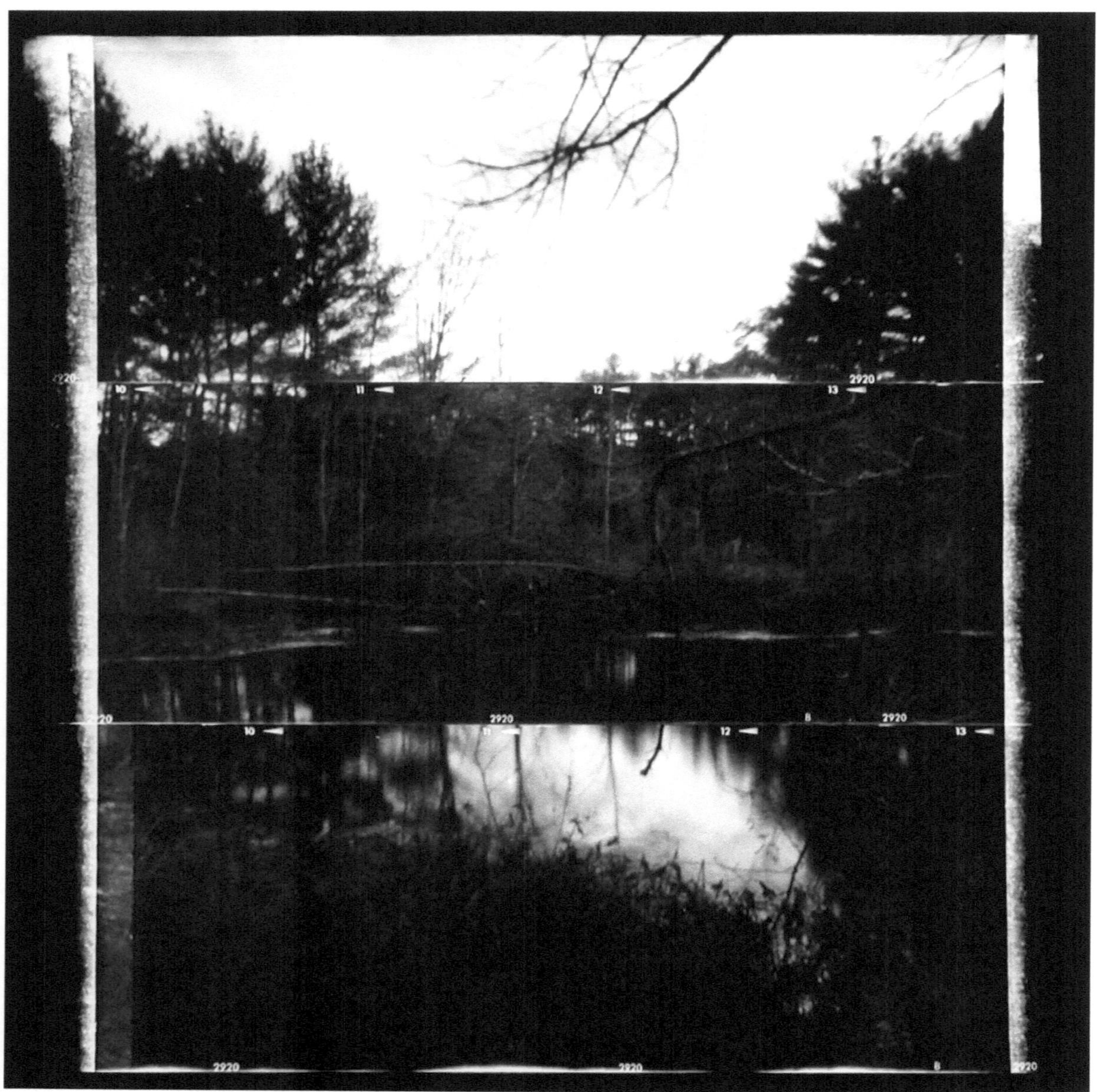
2920
10
11
12
13
2920
2920
2920
8
2920
10
11
12
13
2920
2920
8
2920

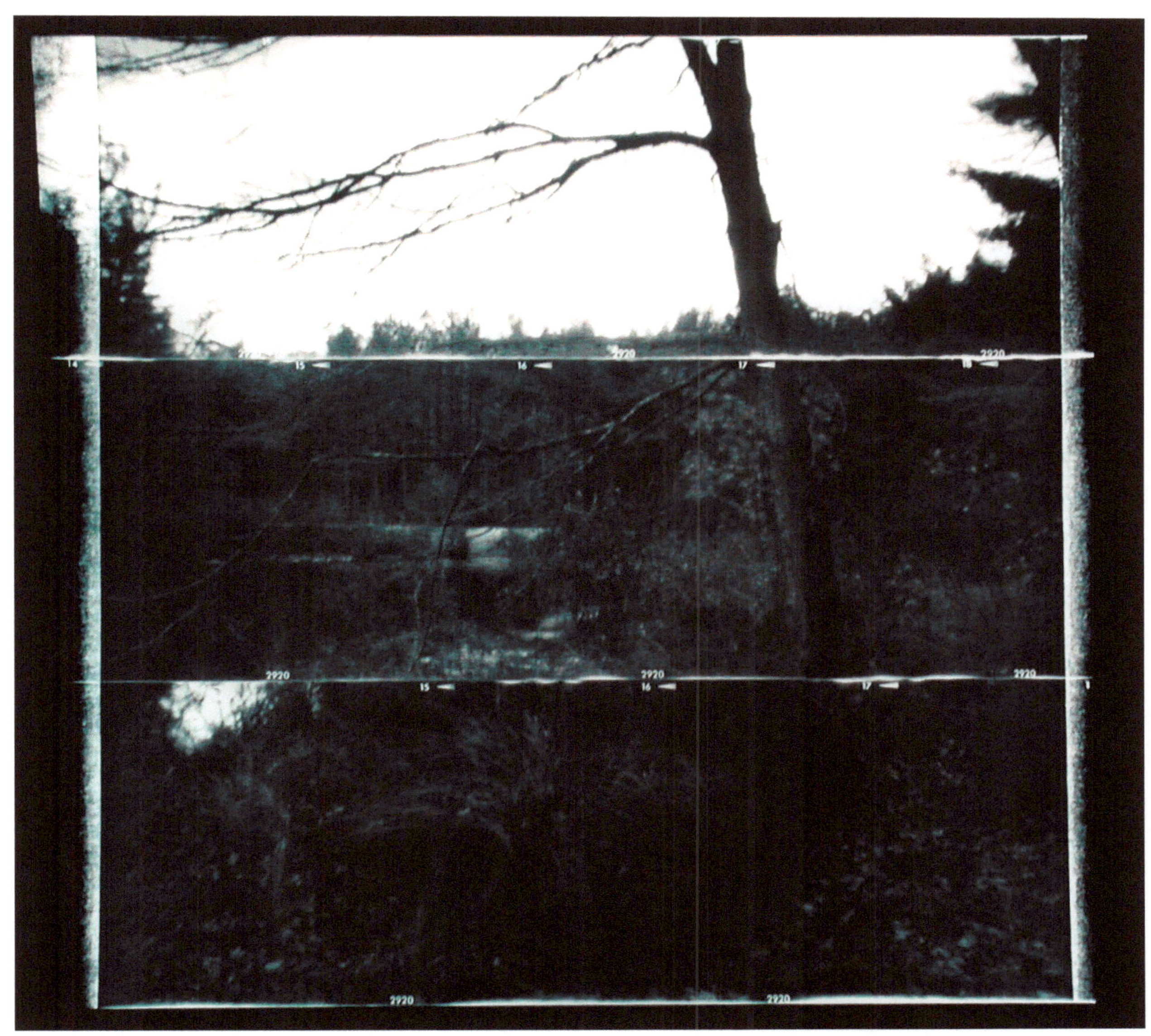

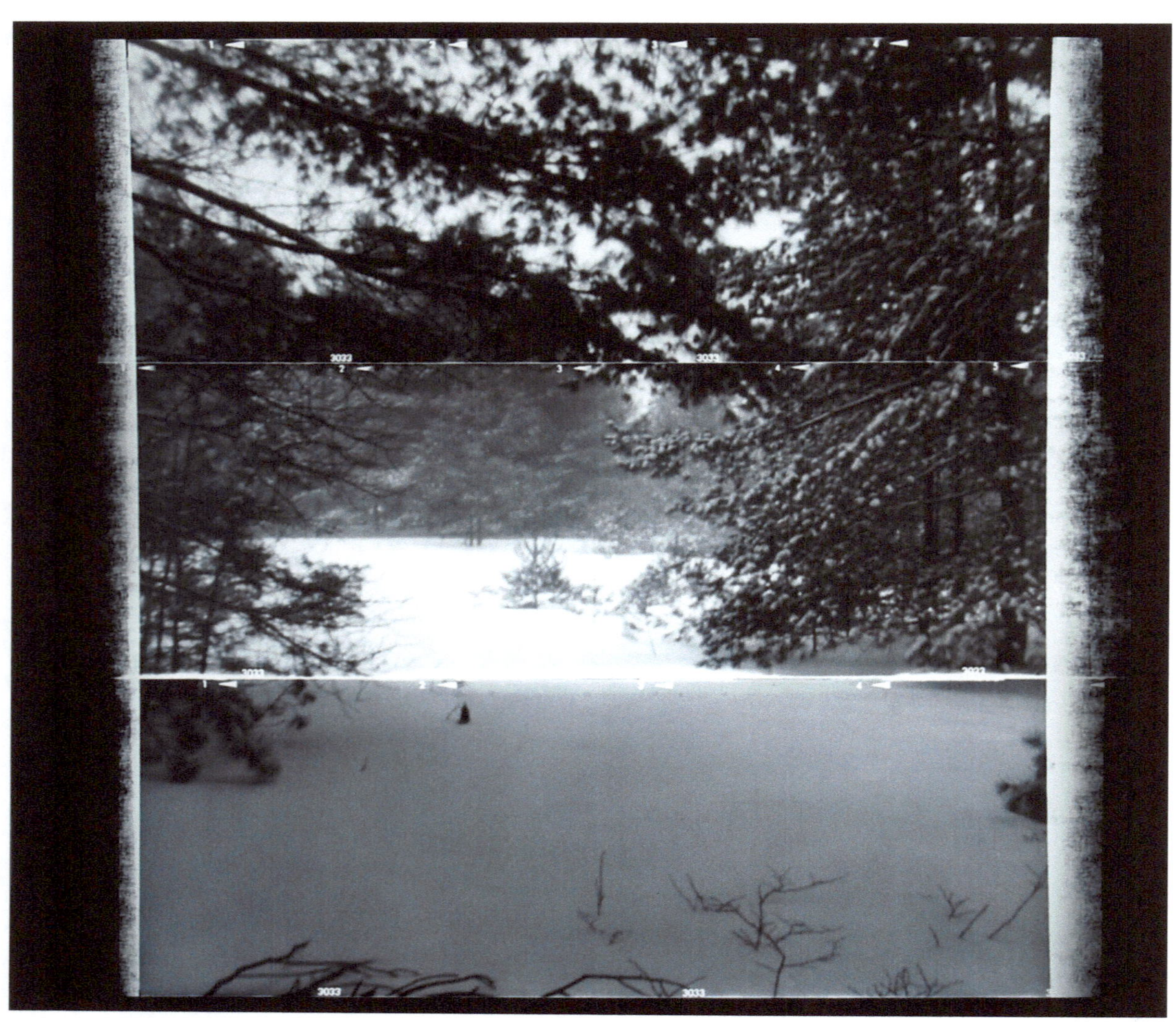

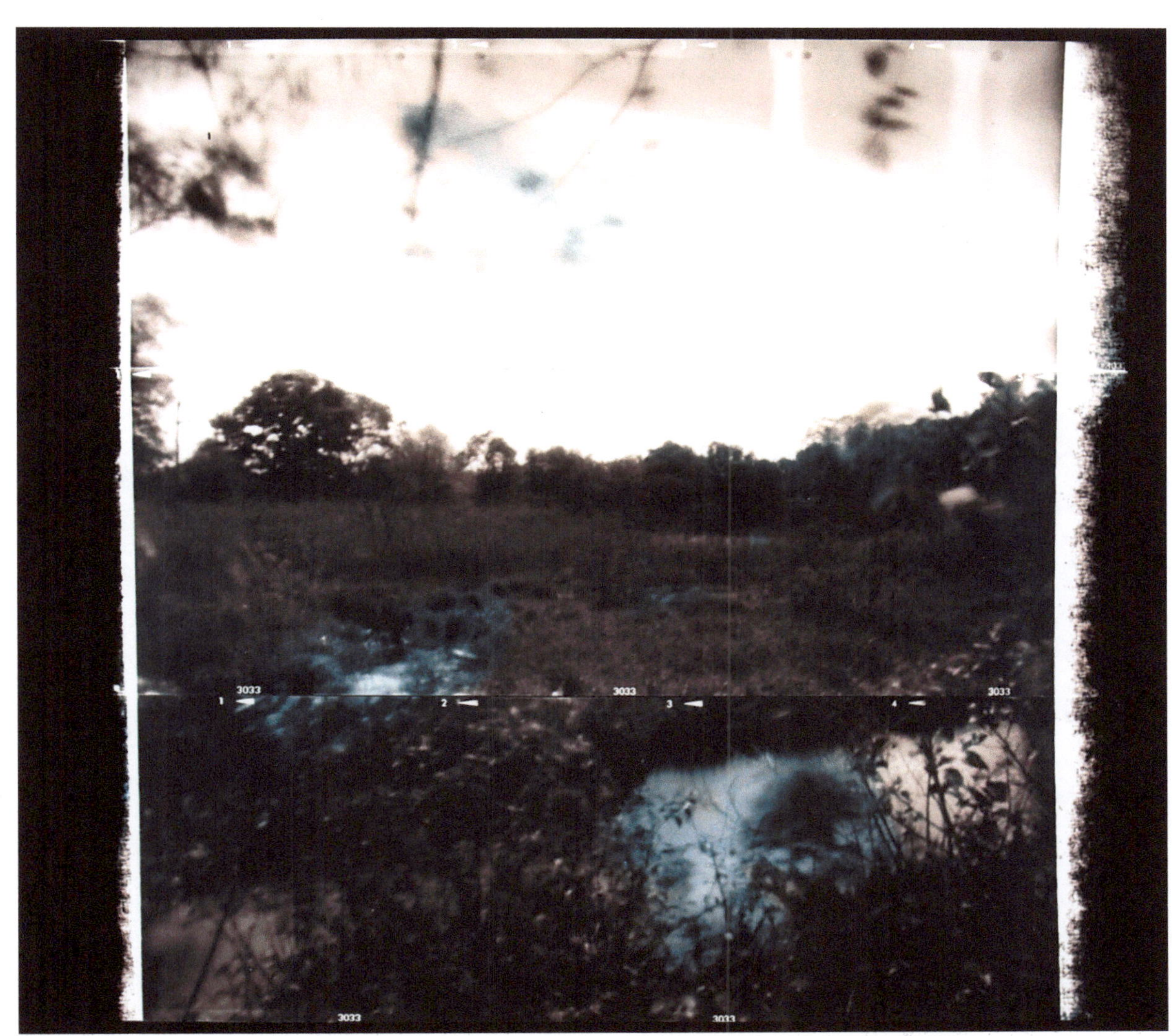
3033
1
2
3
4
3033
3033
3033
3033

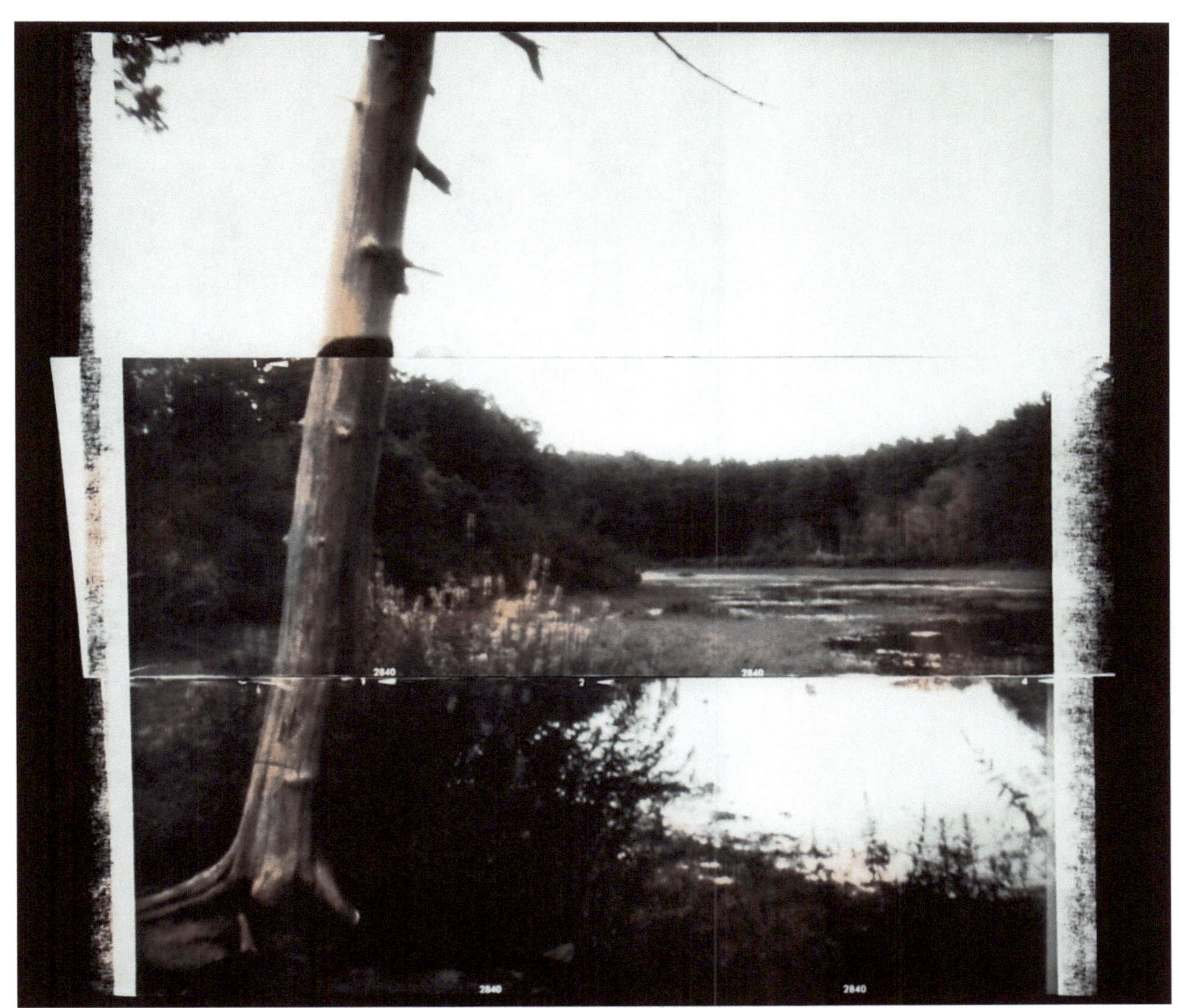

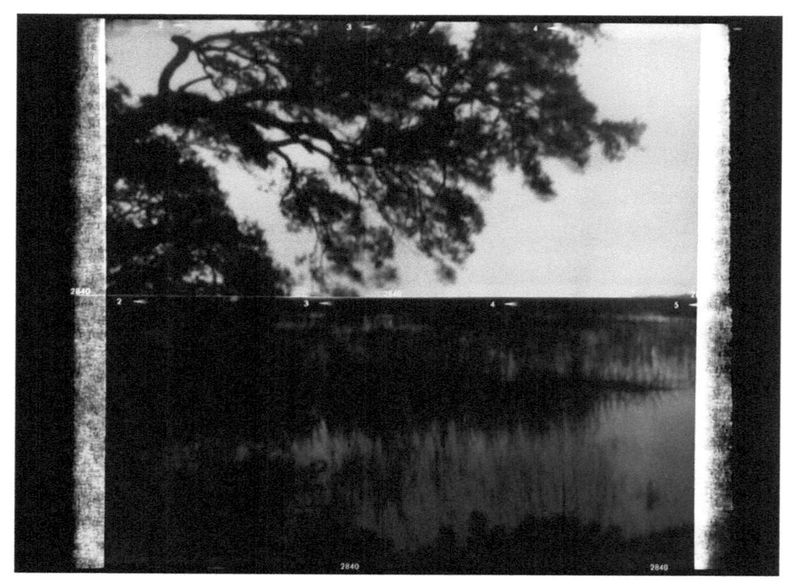

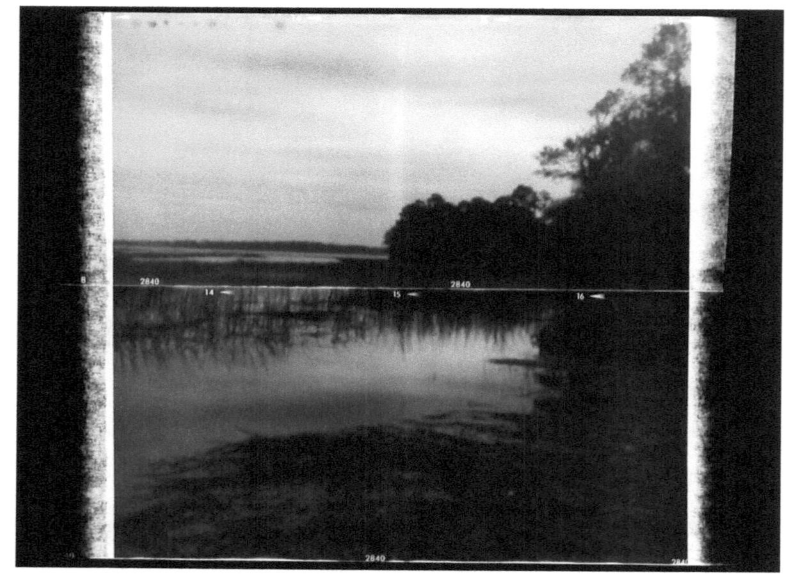

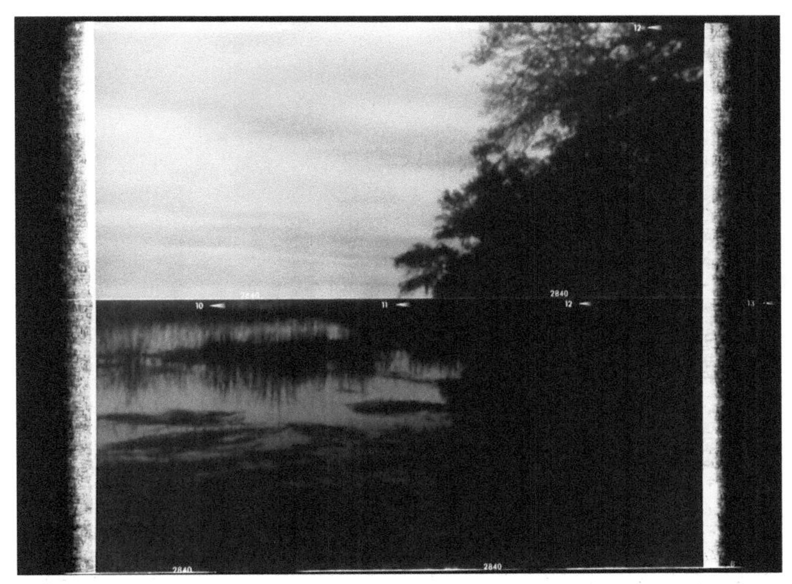

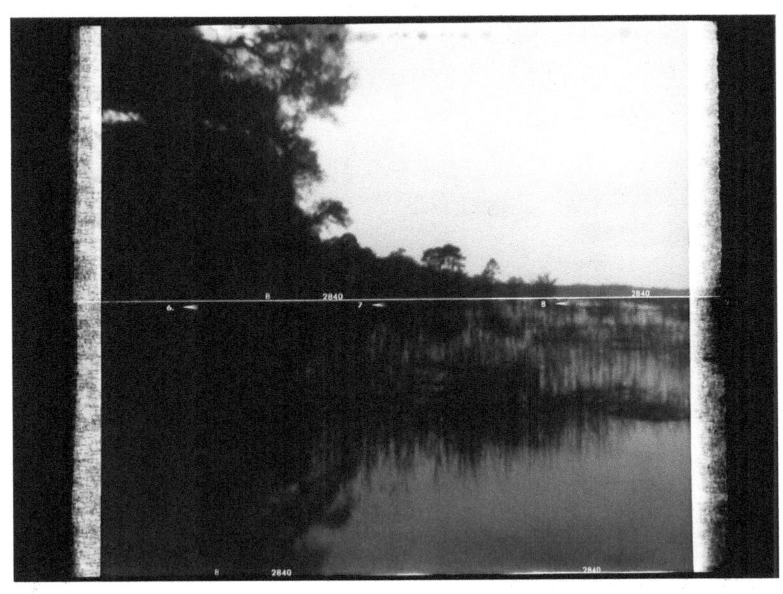

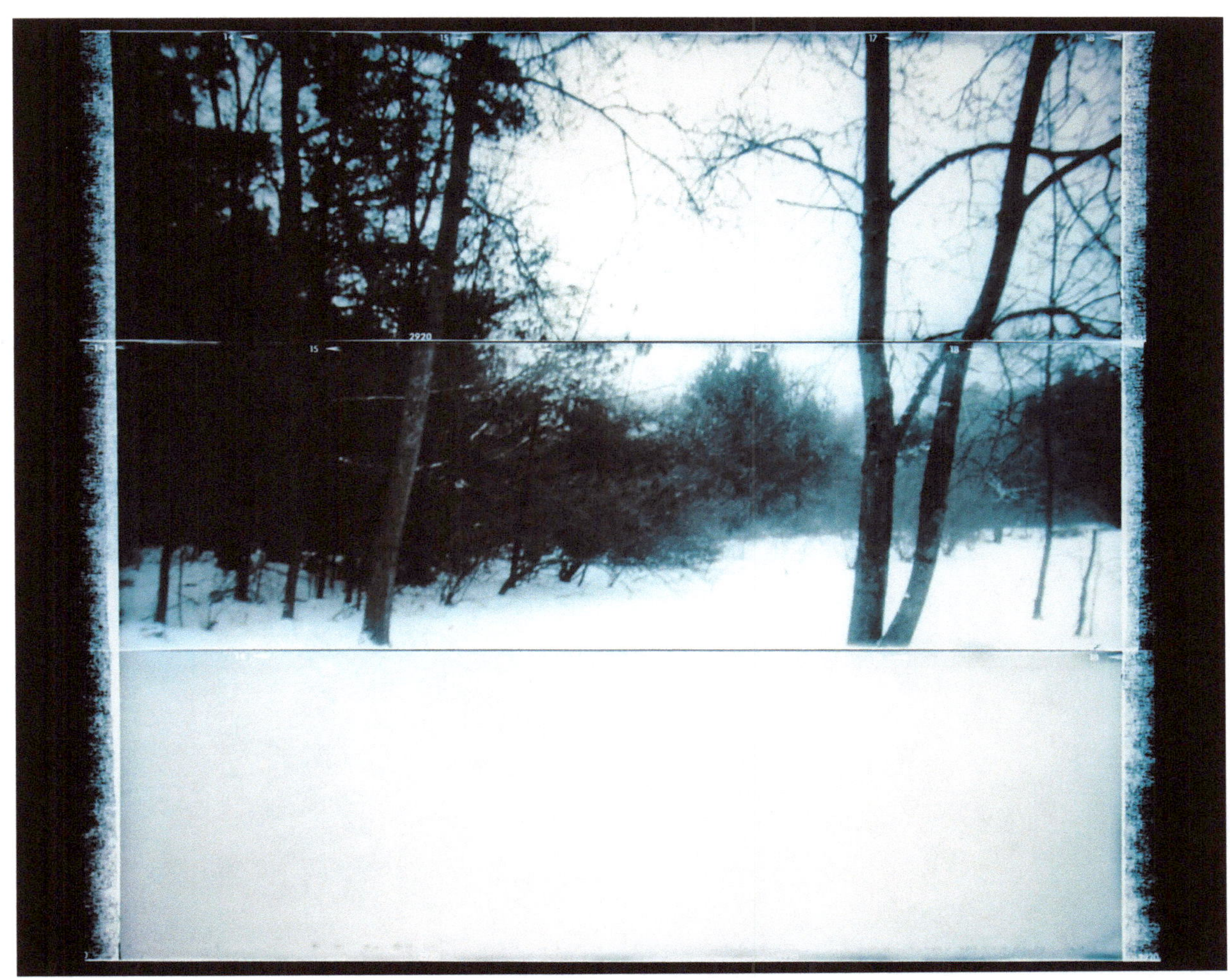

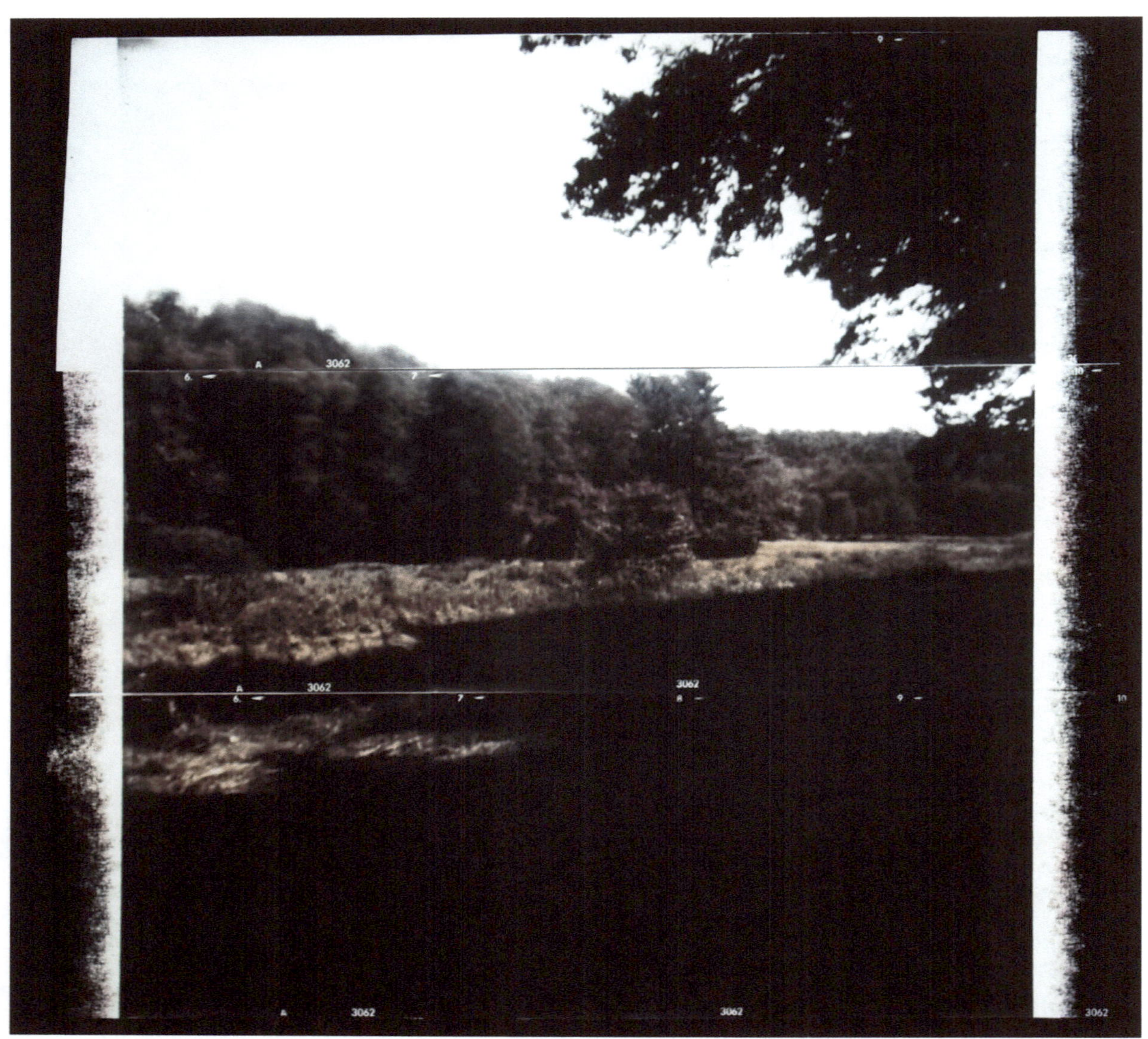

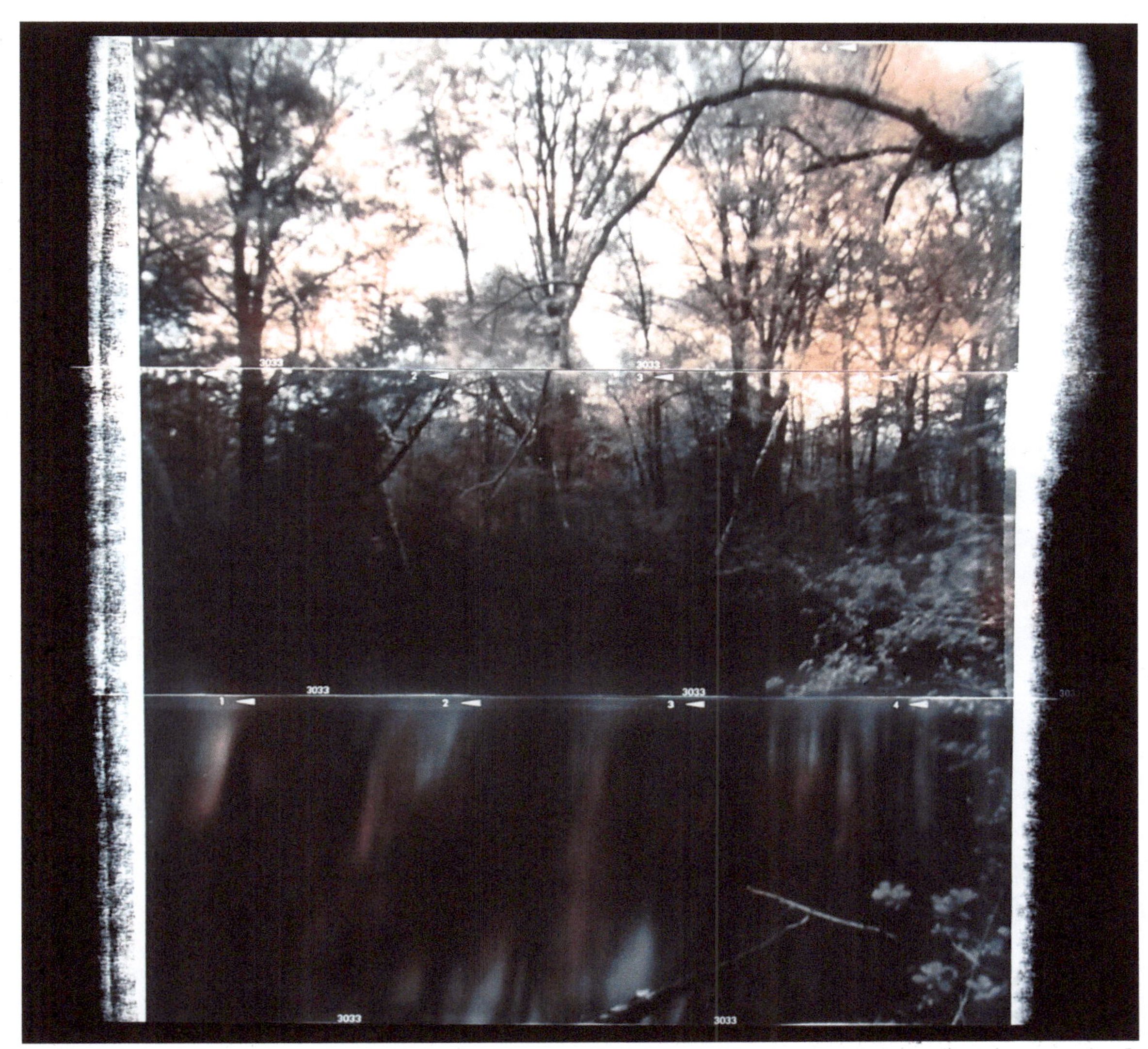

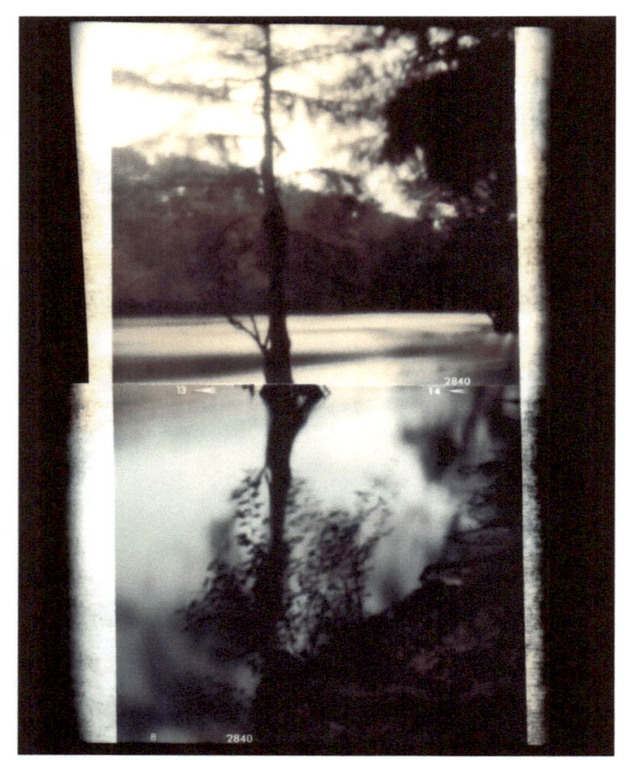
2840
13
14
8
2840

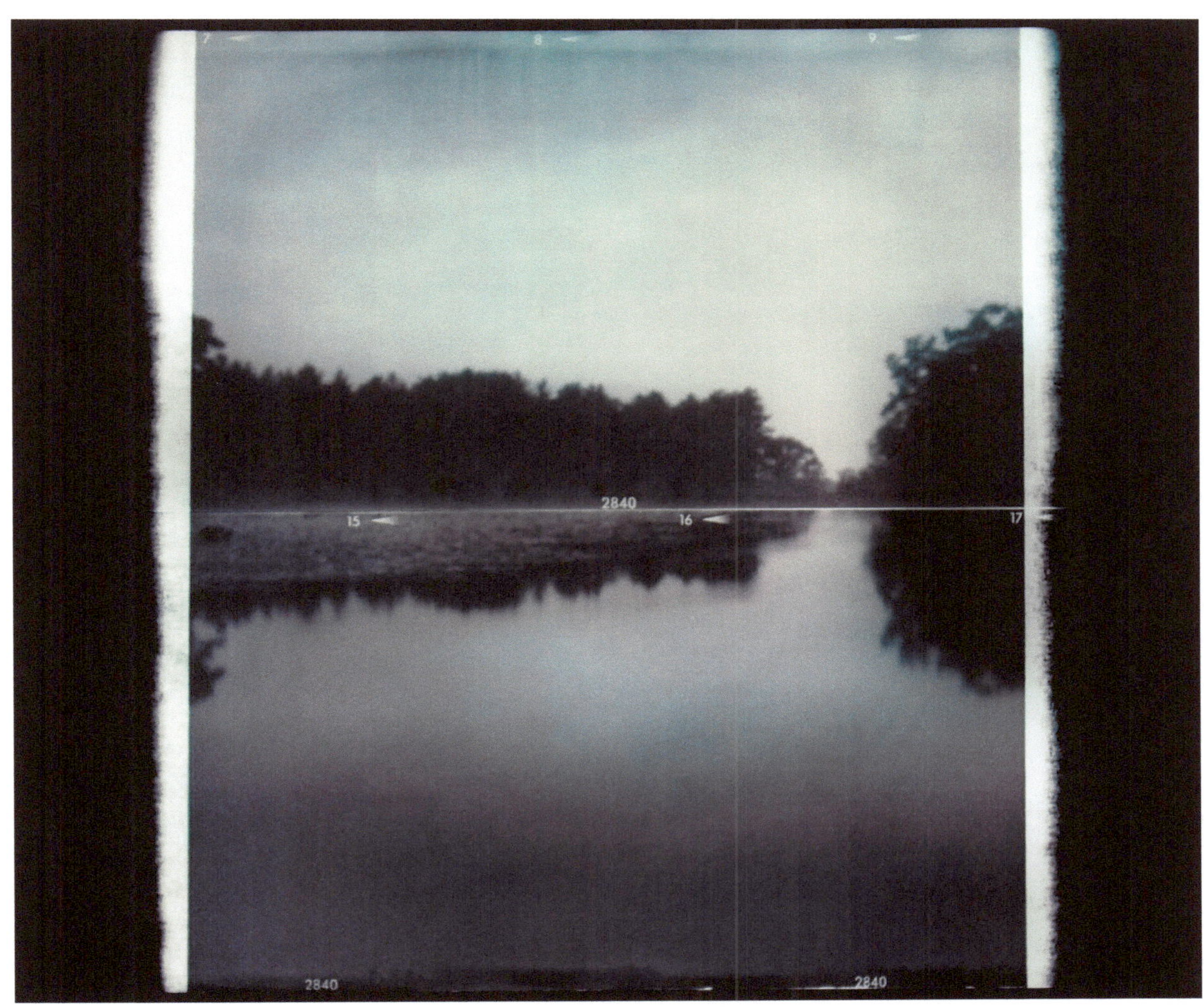
7
8
9
2840
15
16
17
2840
2840

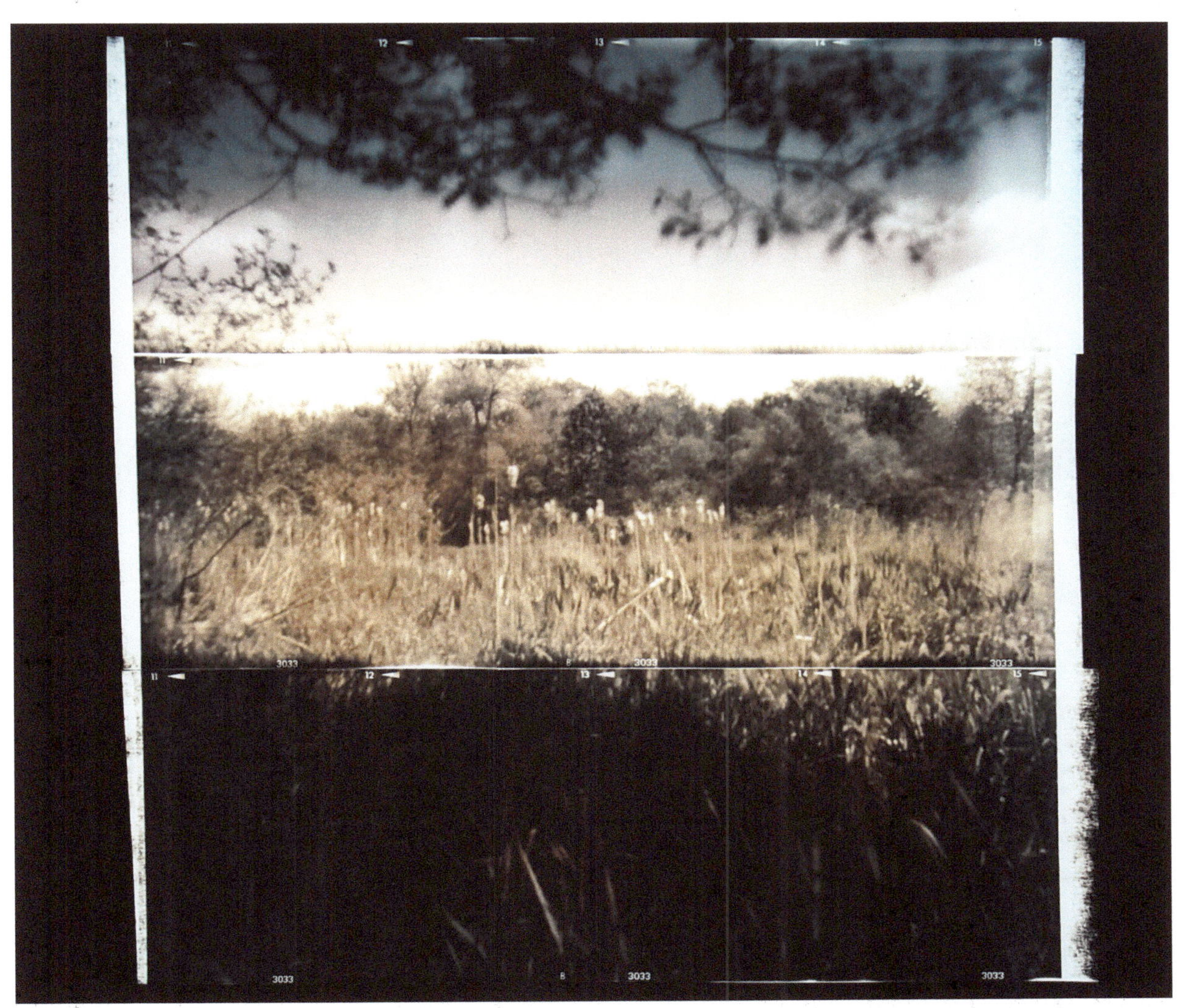

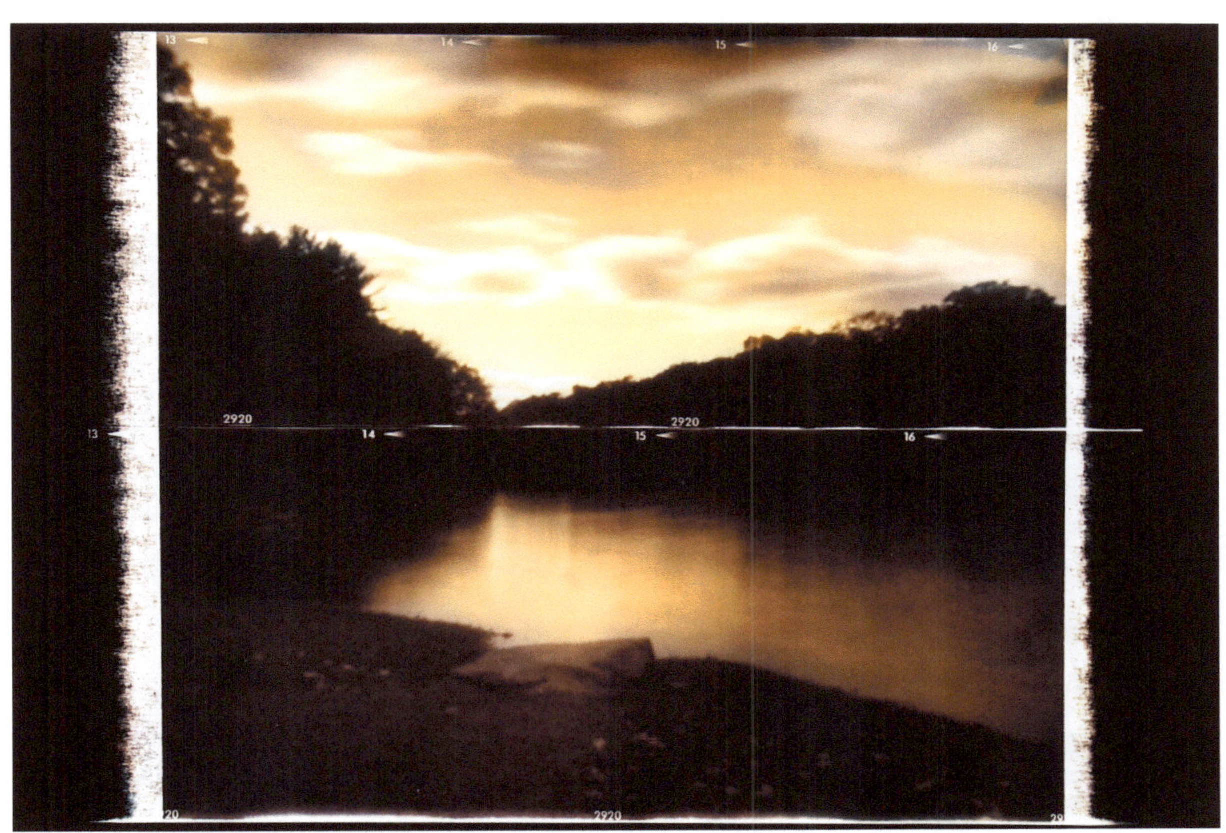

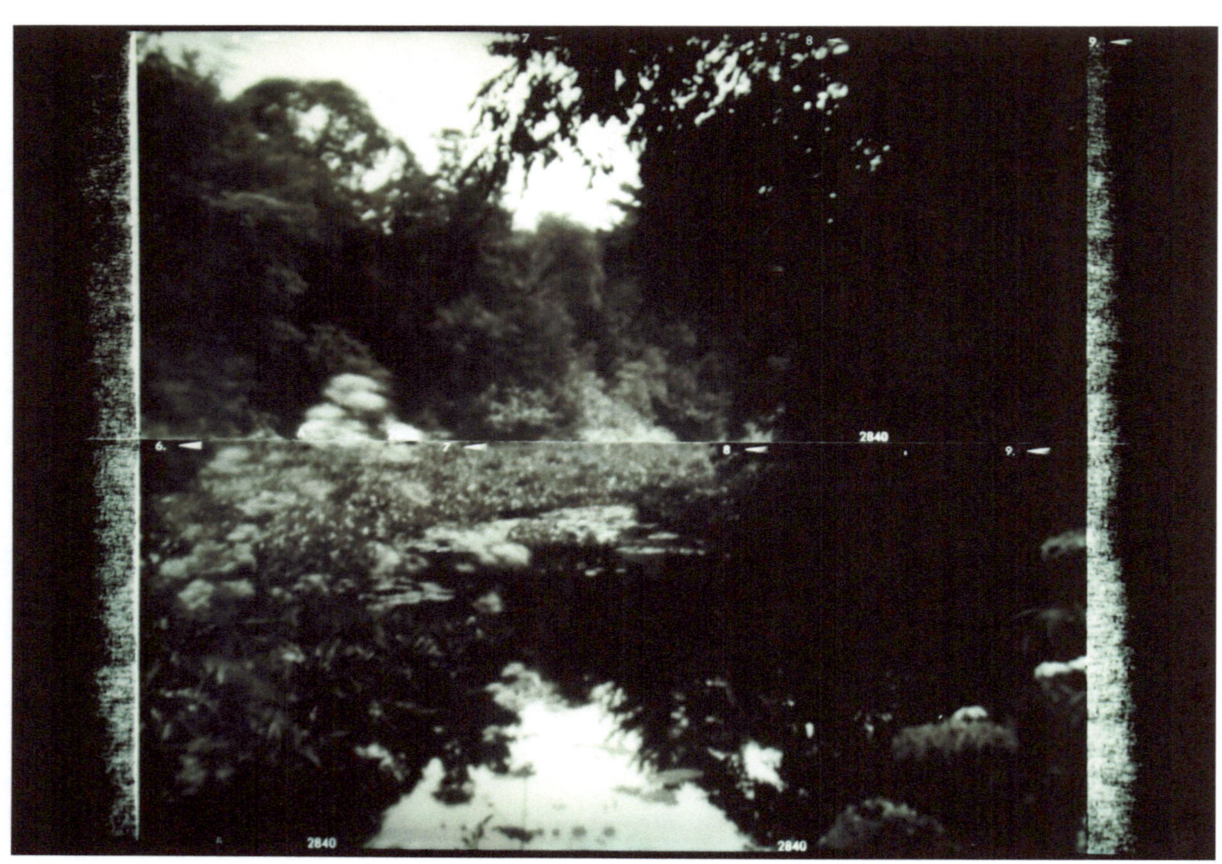

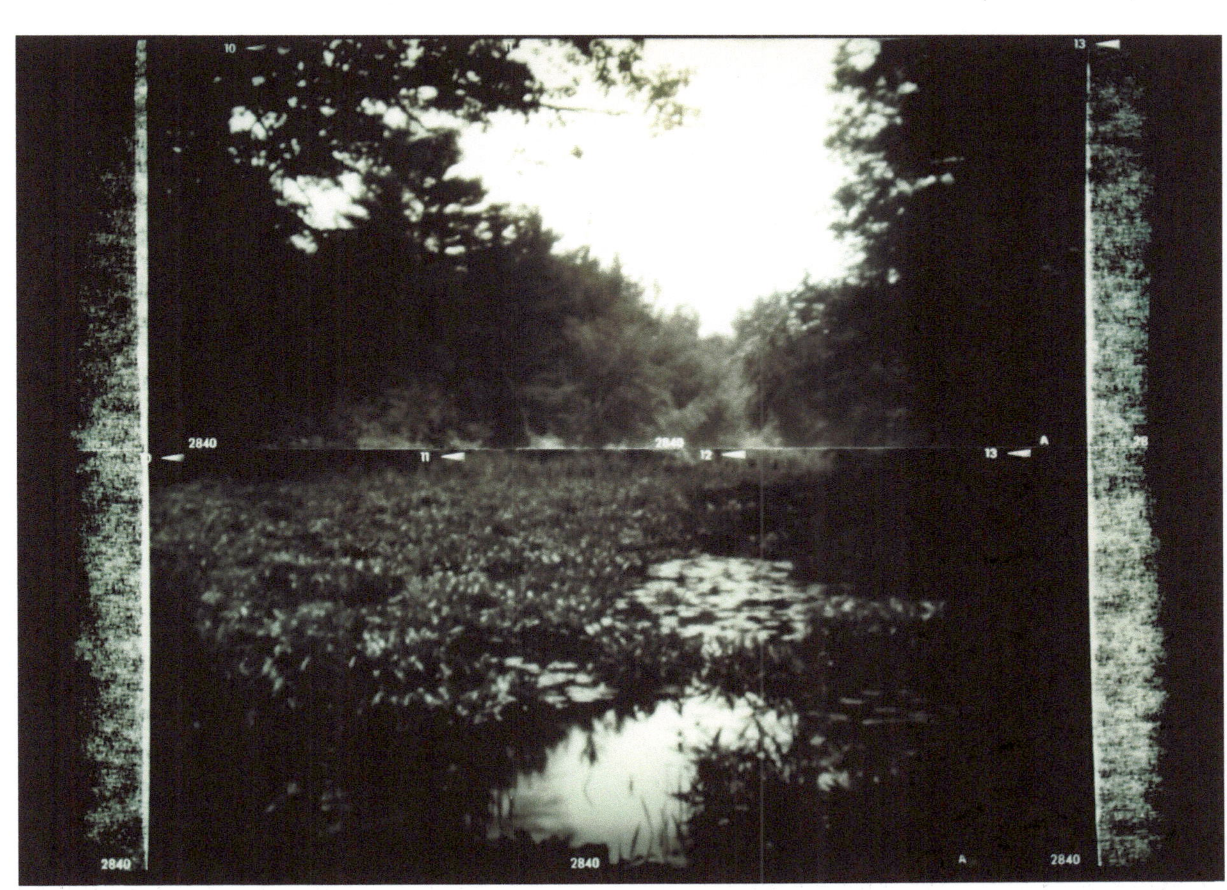
10
13
2840
2840
11
12
13
A
2840
2840
A
2840

My continual experimentation with different cameras and different film formats has eventually led to the creation of my own unique camera that I use today. Through dedication to experimentation my images are works of art that incorporate the medium they're composed in.

The fractured imagery reminds us of the limitations of the medium and the limitations of our own memories. We cannot capture a complete moment of time with a photograph, just as we can never remember a complete moment of time accurately. Humans can only remember bits and pieces of a moment, and as time moves on biases and changed perspectives cloud that vision. Each fractured pane exists in a paradox of harmony and conflict. One moment the pieces are working together to create a whole image. The next moment the pieces are fighting another, trying to capture your full attention.

I began photography in 1993. My friend Bill suggested I help him out with an assignment he had taken on. I've taken pictures ever since. In 1995 two events shaped my career. I took a class with Arno Rafael Minkkinen. And, I made my first exposures on multiple rolls of film. I was testing a camera I had modified. It was a gift from my mother, an antique camera that was originally my great-grandfather's.

I now have four cameras that I have made; two of which are pinholes and two are lens cameras. I have five other cameras that I have modified to take multiple rolls as well. When I shoot, I pick a random selection of three cameras out of the nine to use for the day.

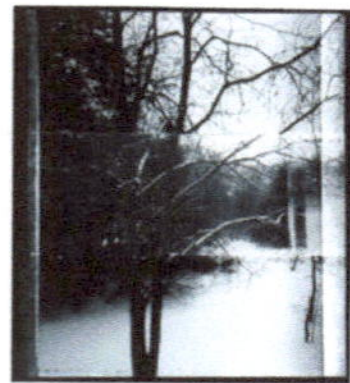
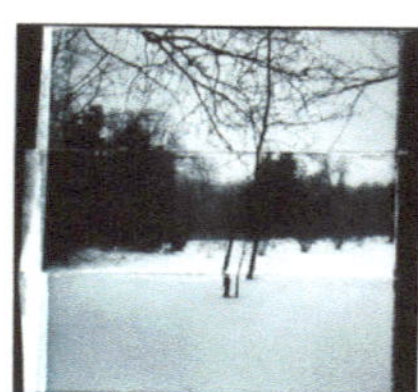
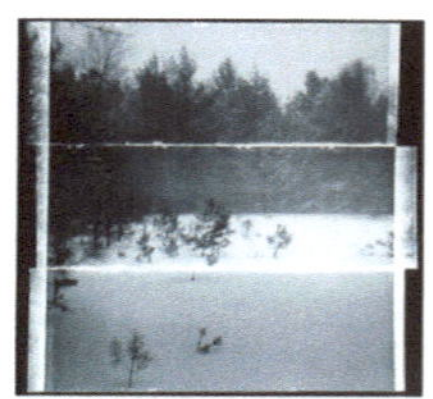
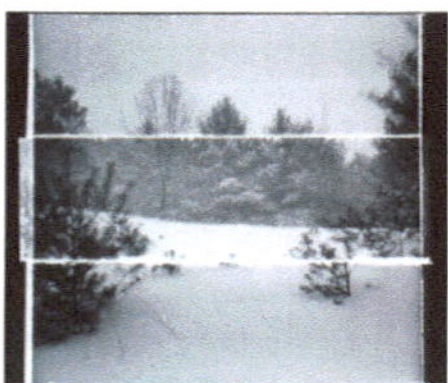

My landscapes reflect my moods. They are an effort to find the "sublime". I hope to create a reality in the images that cannot be mistaken for anything but what it is. A story should have a beginning, a development and an end. A good photograph should not end. It should leave the viewer with something that lives on in their mind and in their world.

I am proud that my work is from a traditional black and white darkroom, from un-manipulated negatives directly from the camera exposure. (Unless you count the tape I use to hold the negatives together as a manipulation.) I utilize chemical toners to add color and evoke emotion. I don't use dyes, color print materials, or hand-coloring techniques in any way. Some prints are immediate. Some take years to realize. I'm still trying to solve negatives from over five years ago.

My work is often viewed as anti-digital, which is interesting given that I have been doing it nearly a decade before digital was in the marketplace. Though digital presents some exciting possibilities, I believe that there are many things still undiscovered with traditional materials. I hope they survive the coming of digital photography. It's already impacted my work in terms of enlarging paper choices. I used to use five different papers depending on the color palette (toners) I wanted and the type of emulsion the paper provided. One has already been taken off the market. I'm sure it will not be the last. Regardless of what happens as long as there is a way to capture an image I will be doing just that with every free moment I get.

-Mark L. Eshbaugh
December, 2005

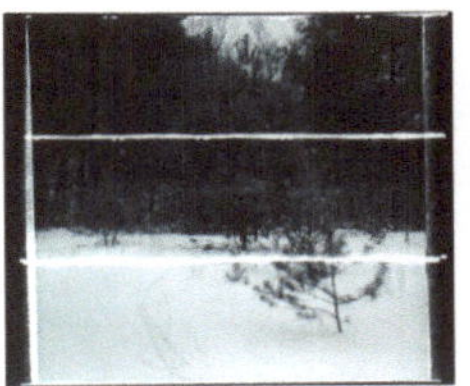 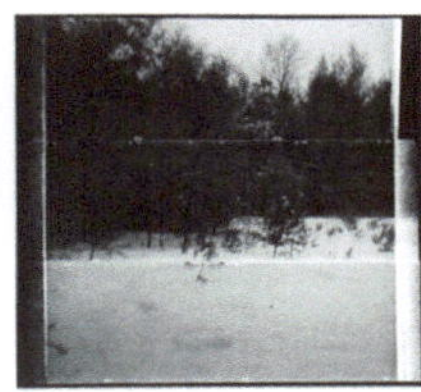 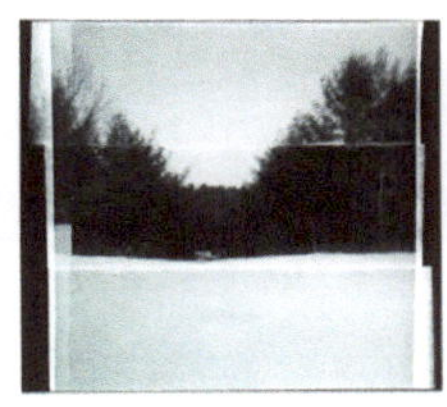 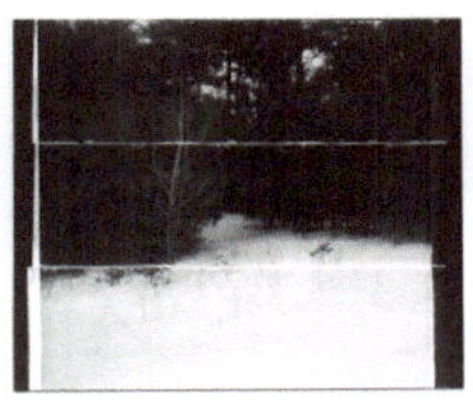 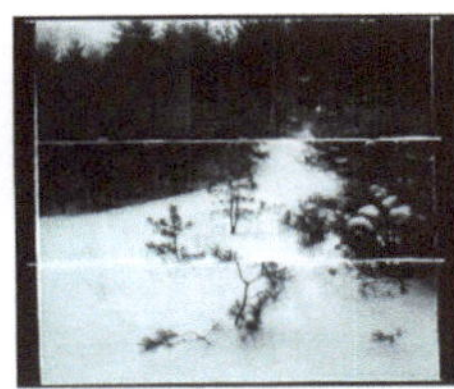

I would like to thank the following people:

My Family, Anne Hopkins, Martha Marsden, Celine Soucy, Arno Rafael Minkkinen, Brenda Pinardi, Steve Mosch, Craig Stevens, Steve Bliss, Pete Christman, Sarah Whiting, Laura Savidge, Terrence Morash, Leslie Brown, Emily Gabrian, Bryant Richards Gallery, Melanie McWhorter, Taeomi and Bob Dooley, Dave Goldstein, Craig Goldstein, Linda Goldstein, Carey Kenyon, Don Tatarka, Stephanie Patsourakos, Ralph and Stephanie Bush, Eric and Karin Karr, Ron and Barbara Karr, Keith, Ken and Judy MacPhail, Bill Turner, Tom and Ann Turner, Beth Parker, Erin O'Sullivan, Kurt and Stephanie Wagner, A. Lynn and Bill Wagner, Beth Murphy Cail, The Durant Family, John Tremblay and Matt Dupre, John Pollard, George and Patricia Pollard, Joyce Bickel, Phil Sarver, Lisa Vivona, Fred Ata, Melissa Boyajian, Heather Szafran, Erin Conlin, Jessica Hosman, The Feineman Family, Mike and Tara Banks, Mike and Jackie Tiano, Jim and Sheila Griffin, Wendy Tape, Alice Casey, Erin Crowley, The Sinofsky Family, Abbey Heaton Schneider, Aprill Aronie, Lindsey Rudolph, John Hames, Mary Virginia Swanson, David Alan Harvey, Dara Emschweiler, Lisa M. Robinson, Thomas Fischer, Shirley Colby, Megan Lewis, Wesley Caunter and anyone I may have inadvertently forgotten.

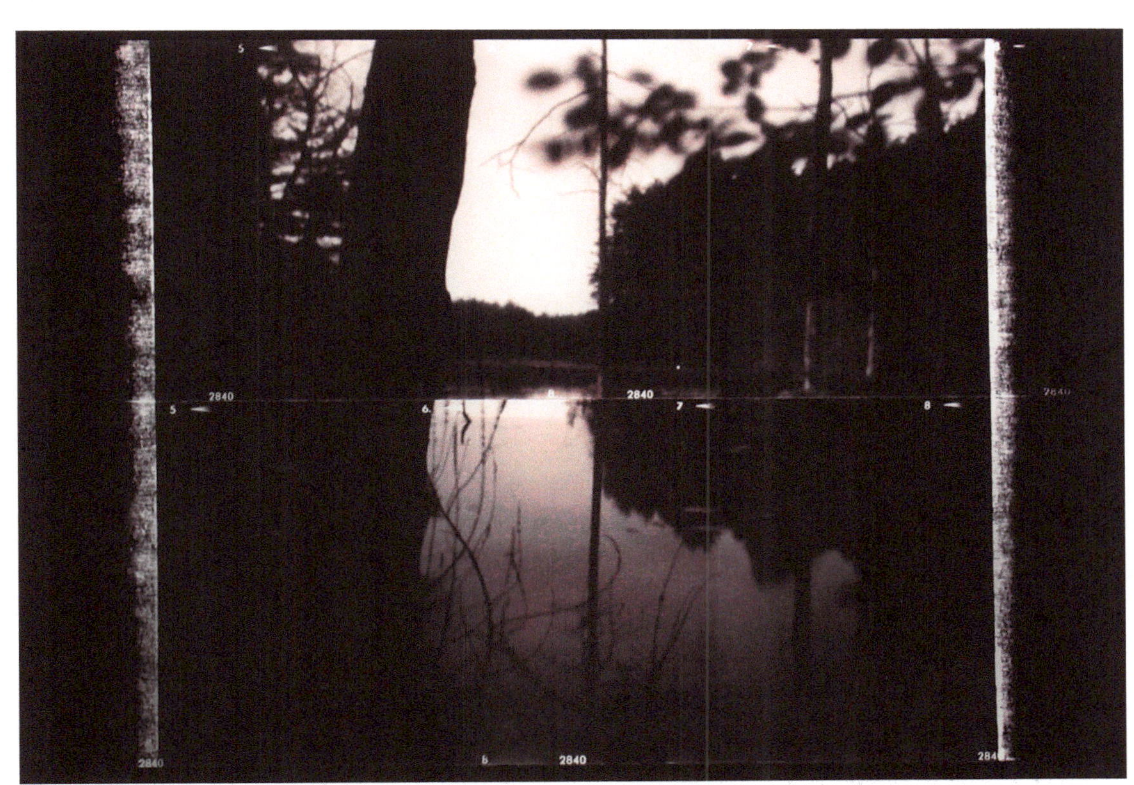

www.ingramcontent.com/pod-product-compliance
Lightning Source LLC
LaVergne TN
LVHW070130110826
845147LV00002B/229

* 9 7 8 0 6 1 5 1 5 2 6 2 2 *